Working Wisdom

Robert Aubrey
Paul M. Cohen

· · · · · · · · · · · · · · · · · ·

Working Wisdom

. . . .

Timeless Skills and Vanguard Strategies for Learning Organizations

Jossey-Bass Publishers
San Francisco

Substantial discounts on bulk quantities of Jossey-Bass books are available to corporations, professional associations, and other organizations. For details and discount information, contact the special sales department at Jossey-Bass Inc., Publishers. (415) 433–1740; Fax (800) 605–2665.

For sales outside the United States, please contact your local Paramount Publishing International Office.

 Manufactured in the United States of America on Lyons Falls Pathfinder Tradebook. This paper is acid-free and 100 percent totally chlorine-free.

Library of Congress Cataloging-in-Publication Data

Aubrey, Robert, date.
 Working wisdom : timeless skills and vanguard strategies for
learning organizations / Robert Aubrey and Paul M. Cohen — 1st ed.
  p. cm — (The Jossey-Bass management series)
  Includes bibliographical references (p.   ) and index.
  ISBN 0-7879-0058-3 (acid-free paper)
  1. Employees—Training of. 2. Employer-supported education—
 Planning. 3. Continuing education—Planning. I. Cohen, Paul M.,
 date. II. Title. III. Series.
 HF5549.5.T7A84   1995
 658.3'124—dc20   94-47379

FIRST EDITION
HB Printing 10 9 8 7 6 5 4 3 2 1

Contents

viii Contents

10. The Managerial Imperative
11. The Network Imperative
12. The Technology Imperative

13. The Imperative
14. The Leadership Imperative 153
Conclusion: Working Wisdom 191
Appendix A, B of Human: Working Wisdom 201
Notes
Recommended Reading 211

Foreword

. . . .

Given: The new economy depends on the construction of value based on knowledge. Given: We therefore need to turn all organizations into learning organizations. Given: We therefore need to turn all workers into lifelong learners.

So?

We are awash in learning-organization hype. Some of it focuses on team building (good stuff). Some of it focuses on linking folks beyond traditional organizational borders, via technology (good stuff). But almost all of it avoids asking (and, thence, answering) THE BIG QUESTION: Just what the heck is learning all about, anyway?

Enter Bob Aubrey and Paul Cohen's marvelous *Working Wisdom: Timeless Skills and Vanguard Strategies for Learning Organizations*.

In his seminars, Bob Aubrey began asking a simple enough question: "Where did you learn what is most useful to you in working life?" "A training course" was almost *never* the answer. And the alternative was not as simple as "on the job." The most effective learning took place courtesy of a nondogmatic mentor, a high-pressure project, a major screwup, or a career change.

Building on this revelation, the authors proceed to construct a model of the effective learning process. It begins with the idea of a journey and an accompanist-learning manager (*accompanying*— the first of five key elements in the model). Then it proceeds through *sowing* (planting the message, probably before the learner is ready to understand it), *catalyzing* (seeking the stressful, "catalytic moment" at which the learner is most likely to have a breakthrough—and nudging her or him to do exactly that), *showing* (rarely achieved via telling, and most effectively "taught" by providing numerous opportunities for dialogue among equals) and, finally, *harvesting* (taking advantage of the prior learning, and moving on to the next stage).

I reread the chapters on each element of the model twice—and both the gestalt and the details grew on me. This is a powerful, profound—and most often ignored—view of the process of attaining wisdom (which is different from knowledge, the authors point out, because it comes through reflection on action).

The book is no dry discourse, though it does go back—without overdoing it—to the ancient masters (even Socrates!) to make its points. But what brings *Working Wisdom* to life is practical examples from organizations around the globe. Everything from an effective federal pen (Federal Correctional Institution McKean) to Johnson & Johnson, LifeScan, and the Commercial Bank of Morocco appear in these sprightly pages.

My favorite was the tale of the Apple France boss, Jean-Louis Gassée. Beset by debilitating contention among top team members, he called in no less than the brilliant, crusty psychologist R. D. Laing. Laing chose to apply "the silent treatment" to the Apple France execs. He gathered the team, asked them why they thought they had been brought together—and then closed his mouth and sat silently. Eventually, the pressure built to the point that the execs began to talk, then bubble, working out many of their problems in the process. The idea of silence as catalyst is ingenious—and virtually unknown to modern managers, the great majority of whom assume they are paid to prattle on and on...and on.

Aubrey and Cohen take the basic learning model and translate it into a practical guide for leaders, discussing in detail the construction of learning organizations and the use of "learning contracts" with employees. They also concoct a new typology of managerial roles—including, prominently, specifically designated "learning managers."

"Wisdom is not passed from an authoritative teacher to a supplicant student," the authors conclude, "but is *discovered* [my emphasis] in a long relationship in which both stand to gain a greater understanding of the workplace and the world." This thoughtful, readable, and energetic book was, for me at any rate, the missing link: what I had not previously found in so many discussions of learning organizations and learning networks. It seems we've been putting the cart (e.g., technology) way before the horse. This book is, make no mistake, about the horse: the deep ideas that underpin the basic (i.e., timeless, as in the title) notion of what it means to learn/gain wisdom in a working environment.

Bravo!

Palo Alto, California   Tom Peters
February 1995

Preface

. . . .

Working Wisdom identifies the most significant resource for developing human capital in organizations—wisdom. This book is intended for people in search of ways to leverage their skills for themselves and their organizations. Our use of the word *wisdom* is not indifferent; we believe it gives new meaning to learning in organizations and best describes how leaders, mentors, managers, and coaches make learning happen. The need is timely: the traditional role of managers has changed, and many of us are finding the new career path a slippery one. Wisdom gives us a point of reference and a culture, a platform for renewing our personal and professional development. It provides a new standard of knowledge and value-creation and offers new ways to understand the potential of an experienced workforce.

In this book, we explore wisdom as a vital and largely untapped resource, a form of human capital acquired through action, accumulated through experience, and applied in everyday learning at work. More importantly, we study wisdom as an organizational strategy for developing human potential in organizations. Working wisdom is what people do to help others learn and what learning organizations do to help people develop. This book is the first attempt, we believe, to provide the conceptual building blocks for wisdom as a management practice and a learning strategy.

Today's management theories and models are evolving quickly, thanks largely to the recognition that continuous learning is essential to the development of individuals, companies, and nations. Some theories emphasize the importance of human networks for coaching and mentoring within the organization, others point to the impact of new technologies, still others propose systematic evaluation of competencies and skills. None, we believe, does full justice to the personal relationships that are so essential to the learning experience and the wisdom that animates these relationships. Why not? Perhaps because it is more comfortable to remain within the secure bounds of quantitative methods and established practices. Our observations, however, have led us to question those limits. We believe tomorrow's management systems will require more than the expertise of traditional trainers; particularly when operating globally amid diverse cultures, organizations will need to tap the wisdom and know-how of those on the front line. This book is an invitation and a challenge to those who will create and work within the learning systems of the future.

Genesis of the Book

The ideas for *Working Wisdom* originated from Bob Aubrey's consulting experience in Europe and his encounters with the diverse and effective learning cultures there. At first involved in setting up training institutes and corporate universities on the U.S. model, he was struck by the vitality of learning he saw outside the bounds of formal training programs. He began researching what managers did in these informal learning cultures and decided to write about it. The book itself first appeared in France and circulated among learning specialists and management researchers in the United States. It eventually caught the attention of editor Paul Cohen, who covers organizational innovations in *On Achieving Excellence*, the newsletter published by The Tom Peters Group. He was struck by the originality of Aubrey's approach in bringing the ideas of philosophers like Aristotle and Confucius alongside current practices from companies worldwide. This rich historical context made the work stand out from what others in the field were doing. Cohen subsequently invited Aubrey for an interview in California, and during their conversation a number of ideas started clicking. They decided to coauthor a new book, with the hope of giving U.S. readers concrete information on how to apply these ideas—and highlighting what companies were already doing to push the limits of organizational learning. This book is the product of their two-year collaboration.

Need for the Book

This book fits into a world where learning has come to the forefront of management thinking, with new publications appearing constantly. Peter Senge's *The Fifth Discipline* ignited widespread interest in the learning organization, and companies have been quick to take up the call. Long before, however, educators had been working on such concepts as lifelong learning and the nature of adult learning. Indeed, Malcolm Knowles declared ten years ago that more had been discovered about adult learning between 1960 and 1980 than in all previous history.[1] Although this claim underestimates the value of traditional paths of wisdom, it nevertheless marks the point at which adult learning became a unified and systematic field.

Had the world economy since the 1980s remained stable and predictable, such research may have been confined to educators and training specialists. But events have precipitated a crisis. In the United States today, no adult can neglect the economic imperative to learn, no student can believe learning stops at the classroom door, no parent can shirk responsibility for fostering learning literacy, and no policymaker can overlook the gaps in today's educational institutions. In short, learning has become everybody's business, and everyone is on both the giving and receiving end of learning. Because of a profound shift in the meaning of work today, each individual is responsible for developing his or her human capital of knowledge and experience to remain employable. In a global, fast-changing economy, organizations must be able to develop their human resources and adapt them quickly just to stay in business. Managers are feeling acute pressure to learn the skills of managing learning and to create new roles for themselves as learning leaders, mentors, and coaches.

Audience

This book is, therefore, intended for a wide spectrum of readers. Some may be looking for practical strategies for their organizations' learning programs. Others may be looking for ways to rethink their entire organizations and reshape them to make more effective learning possible. Here, we think of corporate leaders, adult educators, human resources specialists, and managers responsible for developing others—which is to say all managers having to cope with change. Still other readers will be more interested in how to develop their own potential and take responsibility for their careers. Students embarking on their careers, employees preparing for a career change, and a growing mass of individuals who are self-managing their work as a long-term enterprise commonly ask questions like, What do I need to do to grow in the future? How can I assess my professional relationships? How do I add value to my organization? and What is my future in the job market? This book is written to address those questions.

Overview of the Contents

Anyone reading this book should gain an understanding of learning at four levels: (1) where the learning revolution is going, (2) why wisdom is a paradigm for the new economy, (3) what organizations are doing to enhance learning, and (4) how to assess one's own learning strategies as well as one's ability to help others learn.

The book has three parts. The first three chapters, comprising Part One, examine three revolutionary developments that are changing the nature of work: the need to maintain employability in a rapidly changing workplace; the renewal of wisdom in the shift from the Industrial Age to postindustrial economies; and the convergence of professional and personal development as a career strategy.

Part Two discusses five tactics to be used in relationships to produce effective learning. These are not simple recipes, and we emphasize the need for sensitivity and creativity in dealing with learners. They are actions taken in individual learning relationships, not organizational strategies. Each tactic—accompanying, sowing, catalyzing, showing, and harvesting—is described in the context of practices and philosophies that have best defined wisdom in the past. We offer contemporary illustrations of organizations that have capitalized on these tactics and the reflections of managers who use these tactics.

Part Three identifies six strategic imperatives for implementing a learning strategy that harnesses the power of wisdom. These strategies encompass leadership, middle management, learning networks, technology, public policy, and learning alliances. Each chapter spells out the tasks and defines the roles of key actors in strategic implementation as well as providing examples in leading-edge organizations. We conclude with a summary, Working Wisdom, and an Appendix outlining a brief history of working wisdom.

Acknowledgments

The original version was written in French with the precious help of Bruno Tilliette, who accompanied three years of digressions and doubts as the ideas took shape. Ian Browde made valuable suggestions in the early stages of the English version—and sowed the seeds for our collaboration by introducing the two of us. As our work developed, Hubert Landier in France and Kaoru Kobayashi in Japan provided vital guidance, and our friends and colleagues at

The Tom Peters Group in California offered their wisdom and support. Bill Hicks and Cedric Crocker at Jossey-Bass helped us through the many turns along the way.

We are grateful to Kathy Dalle-Molle for checking our facts and securing permissions and to our copyeditor, Phyllis Cairns, for her sharp eye and keen judgment. These are only a few of our debts; our gratitude goes to the many managers and colleagues who agreed to contribute their ideas and experience to this book. Finally, special thanks to our loved ones—Chantal, Sebastian, Julian, and Charlotte Aubrey, and Carol and Sam Cohen—for giving their support and understanding and for making life so sweet.

We offer this book with gratitude to those from whom we have learned and hope that developing human beings through wisdom will become an everyday activity.

February 1995   Robert Aubrey
                                   Etrechy, France
                                   Paul M. Cohen
                                   San Francisco, California

The Authors

. . . .

Robert Aubrey is an international management consultant with experience helping organizations in over twenty countries. He has been at the vanguard of several management movements of the past decade: multicultural teams, networked organizations, work re-engineering, learning strategy, and corporate universities. His clients represent an extremely wide spectrum, ranging from computer companies in the United States to European luxury hotels to fast-growing Asian companies to government organizations and universities. His work has always been characterized by original solutions to new problems, his most recent innovation being the creation of a nonprofit organization, Metizo, that manages adult learning communities in cooperation with local governments, universities, and private enterprise.

Aubrey left the U.S. in 1971 to spend a summer in Europe as a student of the German language, but a French coed changed that plan and he has been based in Paris ever since. He earned a B.A. degree (1972) in humanities from the University of California and a Ph.D. degree (1979) in philosophy from the University of Paris. His learning experience is not limited to the academic, however: Aubrey spent six years teaching martial arts, and was a language tutor, a corporate trainer, a humanistic psychology dabbler, and even a shaman's apprentice in Africa. Such a wide variety of learning paths provide the basis of his syncretic approach in this book.

Aubrey has published numerous articles in management journals, and three books, two of which were originally written in the French language. With the 1990 publication of *Savoir Faire Savoir*, which won the French Dauphine prize for best business book in 1991 and was published in six languages, his work received serious recognition. His 1994 publication on the end of the traditional work contract, *Le Travail après la Crise* (Work after the Crisis), has already gone into a second edition and has been translated into several languages.

Paul M. Cohen is editor of *On Achieving Excellence*, The Tom Peters Group newsletter. Serving in that capacity since 1989, he has interviewed hundreds of business leaders and policymakers throughout the United States and observed many of their organizations at work. His research and writing spans a full range of management issues, including organizational change, innovation, and employee participation. Cohen earned his B.A. degree (1976) in English at San Francisco State University, after attending the University of Wisconsin.

As a business writer and editor, Cohen has followed a career path familiar to many in the new economy: he has worked for large corporations, entrepreneurial start-ups, and himself. In addition to writing and reporting, he has had a hand in marketing, product development, and employee communication. He has worked in publishing, health care, and the computer industry. Cohen has encountered, from both sides of the desk, the manager's greatest challenge: guiding and mentoring others, often with limited resources and less time. Before entering the business world, he worked as a bicycle messenger, survey taker, housepainter, and stagehand in an international touring company.

Cohen's experience includes sixteen years as a writer and editor for a number of consumer and business publications. Cohen has edited three health care industry newsletters and has successfully launched and managed publications for a national health care consulting firm. He has also managed and edited publications for Atari, Inc. His articles have appeared in the *San Francisco Examiner, San Francisco Business, California Magazine, MacWeek, American Medical News*, and *Health* magazine, among others. He has lectured at the University of San Francisco McLaren School of Business and the University of California, Berkeley, School of Journalism.

Part I

. . . .

Simultaneous Revolutions:

The Changing Nature of Work

1

Learning for Survival

W here did you learn what is most useful in working life?

A few years ago, a young consultant asked this question at a seminar for managers of the French subsidiary of Digital Equipment Corp., a company that spent more on corporate education per employee than any in the country. He thought he knew what they'd say. But to his surprise, no one mentioned training in answer to his question! Instead, they told stories. Stories about how someone, usually their boss, once took the time to help them learn the essentials of their job. About working in teams faced with daunting challenges. About taking on new responsibilities. About failure. About career changes. About personal relationships, raising children, and facing death and how these experiences deepened their understanding of the real value of work. These stories caused the consultant to ask this question whenever talking with people about work. Time after time, he heard the same tales, which slowly led to unexpected conclusions about how people learn at work.

He discovered, first, that the most vital and precious work experience consists of *episodes*. These may be one-time events or long-term processes extending over an entire phase of one's career; but, whatever the duration, they constitute a personal package of experience.

Second, such learnings are enhanced, triggered, and created by the actions of *mentors*, usually managers, who are the key players in learning. And if you categorize how these mentors make learning happen, you can identify the powerful skills they use to facilitate the process.

Third, experiential learning can be *designed* to produce results through effective management. Companies can tap the right resources and people—inside or outside the organization—to support a learning culture; they can identify the individuals ripe for mentoring, as well as the mentors who will share their experience. The transfer and renewal of learning can and must be managed like any other strategic asset.

These three dimensions of management—personal experience, wise mentors, and effective learning—signal a new era in the history of work. We've been hearing the drumbeat since companies started upending their traditional management pyramids in the 1980s: the economy is changing in profound ways, and flexibility and learning are the new keys to competitive strength.

The issues for the U.S. workforce are now clear. Work can be drudgery, an alienating drain of an individual's time and energy, fraught with unhealthy relationships, and building no progress for an individual's future. The sad truth is, this is what work means for millions in the world today, in rich and poor countries alike. Or work can be an enriching experience, a way of developing mastery in the world, a source of valued relationships, and for some—however high-minded this may sound—a path to self-realization. Combining work and learning to promote personal development, as well as a profitable enterprise, is the key. As the pace of change quickens, individuals, companies, and countries that fail to continually learn and adapt to change will be left behind.

The good news is, we have the resources to develop tactics to manage the learning relationship. Part Two concentrates on five tactics many managers use—accompanying, sowing, catalyzing, showing, and harvesting—that are the keys to enhancing adult learning.

Before thinking about learning or tactics, however, we have to have the right conditions for learning. To foster those conditions, we must:

- Give people responsibility to solve problems.

- Design a work process based on change and constant variation.

- Move people from job to job with a progression to ever more complex and innovative work.

- Establish and promote a network of cooperative relationships and project-oriented teams.

- Identify and support the intervention of wise managers in learning relationships throughout the organization.

The Human Resource

The turnover rate of know-how has accelerated. Technological innovations, improvement in production processes, the shift from industry to services, and competition from developing countries all contribute to the need for faster learning. The half-life of learning—the time it takes for half of what you know to become obsolete—has become the key benchmark for career development. For a computer engineer, knowledge half-life is less than four years,[1] but this is also true for production and service workers, financial and marketing staffers, and just about all workers today.

Conventional training, too costly and procedural to deal with the demands of fast knowledge turnover, can no longer meet today's learning needs. Books, magazines, and newsletters have spurred a fast-changing information market promising ever new and improved business secrets, competitive advantages, paradigms, tips, and "street smarts." And the distribution systems that retail learning—publishing, training, consulting, and education—have become multibillion-dollar industries.

At the same time, *learning organizations*—enterprises committed to the continuous enhancement of their employees' knowledge
and skills and to their own collective improvement—are finding
ways to embed learning into their work processes. In effect, companies like Motorola and General Electric are trying to replicate
the natural learning that occurs in smaller firms that prize individual creativity: advertising, publishing, consulting, and research organizations. These information-based companies do little traditional training, because the strong self-learners who populate such
enterprises are simply not interested in passively listening to off-
the-shelf programs.

Brain-based, professional service firms, along with start-up
companies and small firms, seldom encumber themselves with
training bureaucracies. Of necessity, those firms' workers tend to
take responsibility for a wide variety of complex tasks—something
difficult to reproduce in a large company. But today, large companies are retooling their training systems in terms of learning.
Twenty years ago, educational theorists distinguished between two
types of adult learning—university education and skill-based
training:[2]

- University education is defined in terms of the goals
  the individual sets; training is defined by objectives set
  by the institution.

- University education can be judged only in the long
  term; training has short-term, measurable results.

- University education is for use in multiple, open systems; training is for use in a single, confined system.

But learning at work is no longer focused only on short-term
skills or limited in context. In today's organizations, learning is
starting to resemble the university model more than the training

model. With rapid knowledge turnover and fast-changing careers, individuals have become the center of the learning system.

The challenge is how to develop learning organizations. For example, Chiat/Day, one of the world's best known and most creative ad agencies, has radically rethought the basic structure of its workplace, the office. In 1993, founder Jay Chiat stunned the advertising industry by abandoning one of its two showcase Los Angeles offices and reinventing itself as a "virtual" ad agency.

Chiat has abandoned private offices and regular hours, bought everyone who needed one a laptop computer, and made each client project the organizing basis of the company. People now work at home when they need peace and quiet. At the office, they store their personal effects in lockers and take whatever desk is available; by keying in a personal code, they can direct their phone calls to wherever they happen to be working that day. A company concierge provides whatever equipment, resources, or meeting rooms they need. The goal is to structure the physical environment, the collaborative process, and employee development around the creative exchange of ideas that is the heart of any professional service firm.[3]

As a consequence of such changes in the workplace, professional trainers have abandoned the idea they are paid to present, ad nauseam, their products, standing like teachers in front of adults who listen for days on end and then are asked to evaluate what they have learned on vague criteria of satisfaction. Trainers now work hand in hand with managers, providing a service in the field that can be evaluated in terms of business objectives. For instance, 3M, one of the world's best product innovators, holds all units accountable for earning 30 percent of revenues from products introduced in the past four years. The company offers formal training to support that goal, to be sure. But many new products result from the informal interactions of curious people, who are encouraged to spend at least 15 percent of their time working outside their assigned project area.

Back to the Roots

The challenges of continuous learning on a mass scale are new. But the potential of human learning is not. Experience and practice are the essence of many traditional systems of education: crafts, sports, art, and even religion. Off the job, people naturally learn through capable guidance and personal experience, whether it be gardening, piano playing, or tuning a car engine. Creating intelligent organizations starts by applying what works so well in daily life to the *conscious management* of learning.

When people have accumulated experience and mastered a skill, they enjoy mentoring others—and may learn as much from the process as the learners themselves. Often their social or business contacts become a vehicle for the learning relationship. Friends and family members, too, have a significant impact on workforce learning. For example, a study by the U.S. Bureau of Labor Statistics shows nearly as many managers and administrators rely on informal, off-the-job experiences as a source of career training as on formal company training.[4]

Motivation to Learn

Some organizations are successfully putting learning at the center of their management systems. You don't have to be a big company to do this. One of our favorites is Spectra-Physics Scanning Systems, a 600-employee manufacturer of grocery-scanning equipment in Eugene, Oregon, that controls 40 percent of the market. Career advancement for its team-based production workers is measured not by a relentless climb to the top, but by mastery of a wide range of job assignments and leadership roles throughout the plant.

Under Spectra-Physics' pay-for-knowledge Proskill program, workers manage their own training and monitor their progress through a portfolio of manufacturing skills. They are cross-trained by peers in all the skills needed by each team; their proficiency is

then certified not only by their trainer but also by their internal customers. Employees' base wages and raises are tied directly to their
command of core skills and willingness to learn new ones.

Job rotation—in effect, horizontal promotion—is available
only to the top 20 percent of performers, as rated in peer review.
Top-ranked workers are regarded as experts and train colleagues in
production, quality, safety, and materials management. In effect,
Spectra-Physics has created a new learning contract with its employees: the company offers opportunities for job growth based on
the employee's mastery of necessary skills. It is up to the individual
to invest in his or her own growth.

The message, whatever one's profession or position in the company, is that work has become a continuous learning process, a personal investment in enhancing one's job-market value. The task of
managers in the future will be to ask the really hard questions of
their employees: What is the real value added of your work in this
organization? Are you maintaining employability? What new skills
are you acquiring? What learning strategy are you using? What is
your life goal and how is your career related to it? These assessments
should be an essential part of the manager's job, which must include
the continuous development of talent—one's own and others'.

Managing Self-Learning

Ultimately, any learning organization must rely on the individual's
willingness to take charge of the process. To be effective, self-
managed learning requires:

- *Aspirations and goals:* you must be self-motivated.

- *Self-awareness:* you must know yourself well enough to
  manage and improve your personal learning processes.

- *Reflection:* you must examine and question your abilities and competencies, even beliefs and values.

- *Trust:* you must be able to accept feedback and build on it, which demands openness to criticism.

For self-learning to succeed, the organization must have faith in the learner and in the value of the learning process.

In 1980 a group of British consultants and industry leaders established the Self-Managed Learning Program at North East London Polytechnic, a two-year program that leads to a postgraduate degree. They have recently established the Centre for the Study of Change in Covent Garden, as well as offering tailor-made programs for companies like Royal Dutch Shell and Allied Lyons. The programs take as a given that individuals have different learning needs and that learning is more effective if people can take ownership and set their own objectives.

Participants meet for five one-week "residentials" and form "sets" of five or six members, facilitated by a professional tutor and a second-year student adviser. During the week, the sets gather for a "community meeting" and decide on course issues. The meeting is chaired by a course member, not by a tutor. The sets help participants define what they don't know and what they want to learn. The members of the set are responsible for helping their co-members and assessing progress.

First, each set participant goes through a diagnostic phase to determine his or her strengths and weaknesses and to get systematic feedback from colleagues, bosses, and partners.

In the second phase, each member writes a personal learning contract that provides answers to the following questions:

1. *Where have I been?* The response evokes significant events, people who have influenced one's life, and one's patterns of learning. The answer is formalized in a "life line" starting with one's earliest memories and tracing one's successes, setbacks, and learning proclivities.

2. *Where am I now?* One's strengths and weaknesses are examined, and one's general situation described.

3. *Where do I want to go?* One's learning goals, personal aspirations, and needs are defined.

4. *How do I get there?* The program of study one has decided to pursue based on experiences, skills, knowledge, and qualities is described.

5. *How will I know when I have arrived?* Recognition of achievement and how to handle a new position are determined.

The third phase undertakes the range of learning activities to fulfill the contract.

Although many elements of the self-managed learning program are familiar, the big difference is that the learner, in conjunction with fellow set members, defines the goals, the learning process, and the criteria for success. According to Andy Smith, one of the pioneers of the Self-Managed Learning Program, the results in terms of individual responsibility, initiative in learning, and capacity to learn in response to change are vastly different from traditional learning.[5]

In Chapter One, we have seen how learning has become the heart of management and have emphasized that it is not something new: it is a natural activity. Indeed, sometimes learning is at the heart of an entire culture. Such was the case in the fourth and fifth century B.C. The ancient Greeks considered it natural that anyone occupying an important position in society—artist, politician, philosopher, businessperson, general, or doctor—should compete in the definition of values, sensitivities, thoughts, and educational pursuits of culture. Their word for it, *paideia*,[6] means more than either culture or education, because it encompasses an ethical obligation to improve society.

Today, our workplace—where we spend most of our time and energy—is the primary shaper of our life experience. As we shall see, bringing wisdom to our work is not just good for business, but essential to it and to our own well-being. Accordingly, a new *paideia* is emerging, and its vehicle is not religion, politics, education, or art; it is management. Management will accelerate cultural change as it promotes wisdom in the workplace.

2

The Renewal of Wisdom

Wisdom is a personal capacity acquired through experience and thinking; it is also the ability to create learning experiences for others and manage learning processes in an organization. Like leadership, wisdom, until recently, has been regarded as a soft and subjective ideal rather than an essential resource. But for today's organizations that expect managers to promote and direct learning in the daily practice of work, managerial wisdom is no longer an alien concept.

Wisdom is more than knowledge transfer within an organization; it is making sense of knowledge, just as knowledge makes sense of information. Wise people know what knowledge or know-how is needed in a given situation, how to circulate and renew that knowledge by working with others, and how to use it to solve a problem or achieve a goal. Figure 2.1 illustrates these steps.

In terms of skill, wisdom is the mastery of a process, the action that creates an accomplishment, the advice that corrects an error. How do wise people do that? Sometimes they don't have to do anything themselves. Wise people have a profound intuition of what Chinese Taoists call "non-doing"; they find opportunities to *let learning happen* as circumstances demand. Wisdom is an activity focused on the activity of others, enhancing that activity so it becomes a learning experience.

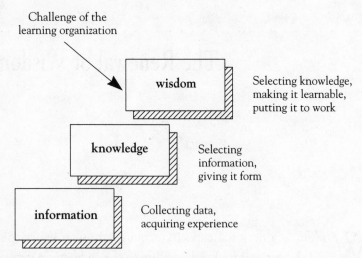

Figure 2.1. Acquiring Wisdom.

Savoir Faire and Faire Savoir

Wisdom is a two-sided coin. Its practical, operational side is the ability to get things done, a way of leveraging experience known as know-how or savvy. Another word for the same idea is *savoir faire*. Through practice, wisdom becomes masterful. Through study, it becomes broadened. Through questioning, it becomes deepened.

But the wisdom that comes with mastery is not enough. The second side of the coin is learning. Wisdom has to be constantly challenged, revitalized, and updated to be useful. Conventional wisdom is not wisdom at all in this sense. To express the learning side of wisdom, the French invert the expression savoir faire into faire savoir, meaning making known. The faire savoir side of wisdom is what is most valuable to a learning organization; it is what one does to make others know. Like two wheels of a cart, savoir faire and faire savoir must advance together; otherwise, the riders turn in circles.

Wisdom demands a new managerial role, particularly now that so many companies have eliminated the traditional roles of manager as decision maker and authority figure. New, leaner organizations make it clear those who are unwilling or unable to develop people while meeting performance targets will encounter tough sledding in today's increasingly slippery hierarchies. Such organizations seek people who demonstrate wisdom in their interactions with others and use them as coaches, mentors, networkers, team leaders, and learning guides. These organizations have gone beyond *efficient* management, which stresses short-term performance, and practice *effective* management, which increases the value of their human capital.

Roots of Wisdom

It is important to remember wisdom has three distinct meanings often overlooked when we think of someone as wise. The first variety of wisdom is *transcendental*, a superior knowledge of the essence of reality attained through study and reflection. In the Appendix, we discuss why this wisdom has dominated Western tradition. The second type of wisdom is *mystical*, an understanding brought about not by thinking but by direct, nonlinear experience. Mystical wisdom can be attained through techniques such as meditation, prayer, asceticism, or trances; but it can also be spontaneous, as a sudden vision or profound realization.

However, a third form of wisdom, *practical wisdom*—what we call *working wisdom*—has generally not received much theoretical explanation in the West. Neither the product of mystical experience nor otherworldly philosophy, working wisdom derives from activity and experience. Working wisdom was deeply explored by Aristotle and later by the Roman moral philosophers. It was also revived as a major cultural value during the sixteenth-century Renaissance. For more, see Appendix: A Brief History of Working Wisdom.

Although it is helpful to untangle these traditional meanings of wisdom, that is not enough. If we seriously accept the challenge of managing and developing knowledge as a vital organizational task, a new concept of wisdom is needed. We can continue to draw on the wisdom of the past. But in the future, wisdom will not be limited to theory; it will be an ongoing activity for professionals in education, commerce, management, and public policy.

A New Concept of Wisdom

We can liken this shift in meaning to what happened when quality ceased to be a subjective concept stemming from personal taste and was recognized as a practice, something that could be defined, assessed, and improved in the everyday work of making products and providing services.

The comparison between wisdom and quality suggests the concept will go through a phase during which it is objectified in audits, strategic planning, and consulting packages. But, just as in the quality movement, we can expect a second phase of debate about the validity of the measurement criteria. Wisdom will never be completely objectified for the simple reason learners give wisdom its value; even when wisdom is sold as a service, it will have a personal meaning in a relationship.

What's new about the managerial concept of wisdom is its usefulness in the practice of learning, particularly in business organizations. Because learning and human capital are of paramount importance in competing economies, wisdom will become a familiar concept in organizations that market learning to clients or invest in developing their human capital internally.

Economic Value of Wisdom

It is not unusual in today's learning organizations to hear statements like, "We must use the wisdom of our people." In organizations that sell knowledge-based services, you can even hear, "That's what our wisdom will cost you."

Fresh thinking about wisdom began in 1985, when economist Taichi Sakaiya published a book whose title is a word he coined.[1]

The Japanese word is a combination of *chi* (knowledge) and *ka* (value), but Sakaiya emphasizes that *chié* (wisdom) is also intended. The word connotes intelligence and sophistication, all of which Sakaiya emphasizes in writing what he calls a "history of the future." The book became a best-seller in Japan, but was not translated into English until 1991 under the title *The Knowledge-Value Revolution*.[2]

According to Sakaiya, we have already moved from a society where materials and energy constitute the most sought-after resources. Possession and mastery of information and knowledge is, he says, the new standard of economic value. It therefore follows in the new economy that is now forming, the life-style that will earn the most respect will be one in which the owner's "conspicuous consumption of wisdom" is displayed, while the products that sell best will be those that reveal their purchaser to be "in the know."

Wisdom is embedded in an object, according to Sakaiya, when it manifests a unique design, is highly specialized, and draws on a tradition or exclusive image. He gives the example of a necktie with a designer trademark like Hermès or Dunhill that sells for five times the price of a similar necktie made of the same material and possibly manufactured in the same factory. The "wisdom" or "chika" is the security and recognition the wearer enjoys by being in the know about fashion. Sakaiya accepts, of course, that such products have always existed, but believes they will embody the economic value of most goods and services. "In the knowledge-value society that is emerging, such valuation will no longer be the exception but the rule; it will not be the occasional product that commands a high price because it has knowledge-value; virtually all products will be evaluated on this basis. It will be the standard rationale understood and acknowledged by everyone, the assumption on which the social structure is founded and in accordance with which individuals behave."[3]

We believe wisdom has an obvious place in business; and indeed, as we approach the twenty-first century, the specific know-how, skills, tools, processes, and learning systems already constitute a major industry. Although the new technologies of simulation, learning games, interactive video, and others may deliver information and possibly knowledge, they do not provide wisdom. The key to educating adults remains the mentors and managers who guide the learning process and give meaning to learning goals.

Leadership and Wisdom

In fifth-century B.C. Athens, Pericles instituted democracy as a form of government and led his city-state to cultural glory. Pericles persuaded free Athenians to build Greece's greatest architectural testimony to beauty, the Parthenon, where no slave would lay a stone. The act was accomplished not only through the wisdom of a leader but also of the citizens who actively participated in democratic government and cultural achievement. Such is the wisdom leaders need to transform our organizations.

In contemporary organizations, we can find many instances of wise leadership in advancing innovative strategies for developing people. Consider these examples.

• In Morocco, Abdel Aziz el Alami built the Commercial Bank of Morocco, the country's largest private bank. He invented the minibank, a commercial branch office composed of only three people that became the key to the striking international growth of the company. Aziz also systematically promoted women to managerial positions in an Islamic country where fundamentalist customs would have them wearing veils and staying at home. But the clearest indication of Aziz's particular brand of managerial wisdom goes beyond employee development and the growth and profitability of his own bank; it extends to Moroccan culture itself, particularly in defending an open society. He illustrated his commitment during a conversation in Casablanca on December 13, 1990, the day before street riots left eleven people dead. To conclude our interview, Aziz asked for a piece of paper and wrote the following poem:

They told me: take care of yourself first;
I replied: let life bring what it may.
They told me: men are to be used;
I replied: I know many who are excellent.
They told me: women are worthless;
I replied: they have done me much good.
They told me: you are too generous;
I replied: one is never good enough.
They told me: you are a fool;
I replied: and may I so remain![4]

• Microsoft, famous for its growth and market domination, has made clear that its continued success depends on maintaining the learning edge. Bernard Vergnes, president of Microsoft Europe, says this about how he judges Microsoft managers: "A manager has a mission to make people better, at all times and in all circumstances. One offers one's work in service to others, and one should always ask what one's work signifies. The key question for a manager is, 'Does my work make others more intelligent?'"[5]

• Konosuke Matsushita, founder of Matsushita Electric, was one of the century's wisest business leaders. As early as 1946, he established Peace and Happiness through Prosperity, an institute whose mission was to study different cultures, sponsor management seminars, and publish books and periodicals. Its three guiding principles are "learn from the past, tap collective wisdom, and promote the union of theory and practice." In 1987, at the age of 93, Matsushita wrote about the role of wisdom in today's society: "At this critical juncture in the history of our civilization, we need to get back our confidence in the essential rightness of human wisdom. . . . Wishful thinking is useless, and platitudes about peace are mere verbiage. What we need is action derived from concerned optimism and collective wisdom if we are to bequeath a happy, peaceful world to our children and grandchildren in the 21st century."[6]

....

• Rosemarie B. Greco, president and CEO of CoreStates Bank, began her leadership role in banking when she was unexpectedly asked to take over branch banking at First Fidelity. Before meeting her new boss, she wondered what kind of manager First Fidelity was looking for. Greco, a former nun who had taught school and started at the bank as a secretary, certainly didn't fit the profile of the managers she replaced. That is exactly why her new boss chose her; as she recounts, "I reminded our new CEO that I hadn't worked in the branches since my secretarial days, had never been a branch manager, and obviously had never made a commercial loan. His unforgettable response was, 'You can learn the business. I need you to teach the people how to change.'"[7]

Although necessary, leadership is not enough to create a learning organization. Learning leaders do more than inspire: they set specific development targets for their organizations and get personally involved in helping people learn. But they need the help of the wisdom that is distributed throughout the organization.

Coaches, Mentors, and Learning Guides

The classical roles of managers—hierarchical figure, supervisor, and functional expert—are being revamped or eliminated as workers and teams assume more managerial functions. This has left managers with an obligation to transform themselves within the organization and establish learning relationships to replace authoritarian relationships.

Organizations look to coaches, mentors, and learning guides to animate their learning strategies.

Coaching is usually a hands-on, skill-related learning relationship, while mentoring is based on personal advice and career guidance. Laurent Daloz gives a good definition of a mentor: "The mentor seems to manifest for protégés someone who has accomplished the goals to which they now aspire, offering encouragement and concrete help."[8] The expression "learning guide" is less common but describes the process of accompaniment in an individual learning relationship.[9] For example, reengineering designates a leader and a "process owner" responsible for guiding people through the learning cycle.[10]

At first blush, these functions may seem to have little to do with wisdom because the learning process is often task-oriented. But that doesn't mean the relationship is limited to the task. Whenever a person takes on the responsibility of a learning relationship, he or she is inescapably involved with the most noble part of working with people, as David Boulton, president of the software company Diacom Technologies, reminds us:

> I see the mentor in the richest sense as somebody who is dancing around the edge of a human being, extending his or her being and who at the same time has the wisdom to be a facilitator. The quality of that presence is "weightless"—that is, not loading the learner down with ideas of what to learn or when. It's not possible to engage in a real dialogue except to come in weightlessly, otherwise the mentor relationship is drawing the learner onto a path other than his own. The mentor has to be learning also, so the relationship is one of mutual buoyancy. The mentor should be open to whatever comes up in the learning process.[11]

Skills of Wisdom

The skills of wisdom include what leaders, mentors, and managers do to make learning happen in a given situation.

We identify five key learning-management skills or tactics inherent in adult learning. Each specific activity is to be used in a context of learning, often requiring psychological insight, sensitivity, and creativity. These skills are valid in diverse learning organizations and are not limited to business. They span historical periods and cultural boundaries and are particularly valuable in culturally diverse environments. They can be found in many philosophies and education theories of the past and have even been the basis of specific institutions that have left their mark on the history of learning.

Figure 2.2 shows an evolutionary progression indicating the relationship between the skills of wisdom and an individual learning cycle. The learning cycle could also be represented as a circle because the work of the manager begins again and again with different individuals and multiple learning cycles. Or the image could be represented as a spiral to indicate the learner never really returns to the same point, but repeats the process at different levels for different types of learning and at different stages of career development.

Defining the Skills of Wisdom

We define the five skills of wisdom in terms of everyday workplace activities:

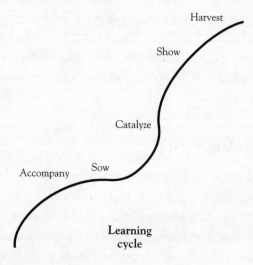

Figure 2.2. Skills of Wisdom.

Accompany. The reason we cannot do without learning guides in today's organizations is the need for human presence and commitment in learning. A caring person must be present as the learner progresses. Accompanying involves taking part in the learning process by taking the path with the learner.

Sow. Learning guides, coaches, and mentors are often confronted with the difficulty of preparing the learner before he or she is ready to change, and leaders have the same problem changing an organization. Sowing is necessary when you know what you say may not be understood or even acceptable to learners at first, but will make sense and have value to the learner when the situation requires it.

Catalyze. When change reaches a critical level of turbulence or chaos, a new order must emerge. Here, the learning leader or mentor plunges the learner right into change, provoking change, accelerating its course, and using it as a learning tool.

Show. Making knowledge visible and intellectually understandable is necessary, as is providing leadership or a role model to embody a skill or activity. Showing involves more than the abstract representation of knowledge. At the dialogue level, showing also means revealing oneself to others and showing what one believes.

Harvest. The final stage of the learning cycle occurs when the learning guide, coach, or mentor focuses on bringing to light the learner's ideas or skills, assesses them, and helps define how they will provide the most value to the organization. This skill we call harvesting. The key questions are, What have we learned? How valid is it? and How can it be used?

In varied and subtle ways, managers must combine and leverage these five skills according to the needs of the learner and the organization. The skills are neither isolated nor merely mechanical methods. That is why wisdom is needed to implement learning.

No leader, mentor, or coach is an expert in all these skills; thus, organizations must provide resource networks to put the people with the skills of wisdom in contact with one another. In other words, there are two kinds of learning management: one consists in personally helping people to learn; the other consists in knowing who can help you make learning happen.

You may wonder, Why these five skills? There must certainly be others and, in any case, how do we know these are the essential ones? It would be foolish to claim these skills are the definitive pieces to a puzzle. This five-part framework is not a rigid model; rather, it is a way of understanding the subtle and largely unconscious process by which adults learn. The learning process does not follow a strict, linear methodology. In fact, the most profound learning usually unfolds through unplanned, unscripted, and untidy episodes. It does, however, require a personal and organizational commitment to institutionalize opportunities for learning as a part of work life. That, in turn, demands individual employees be responsible for their own development—and learning managers be accountable for supporting the development of others.

An illustration of how several skills can be combined as a learning tactic is beautifully captured in Peter Drucker's story of watching the famous musician and conductor Arthur Schnabel conduct a lesson for a promising young student:

> Schnabel pulled out her assignments for the next lesson, a month hence, and had her sight-read them. Again the technical competence of the young woman was noticeable.... Then, however, he went back to the two pieces she had practiced the month before and played earlier. "You know, my dear Lilly," he said, "you played those two pieces very well indeed. But you did not play what *you* heard. You played what you think you should have heard, and that is faking. And if I heard it, an audience will hear it too." Lilly looked at him, totally baffled. "I'll

tell you what I'll do," said Schnabel. "I will play the Andante of the Schubert sonata the way *I* hear it.... You
listen to what *I* hear, and then I think *you* may hear."

Schnabel sat down at the piano and played the
Schubert Andante the way he heard it. Suddenly
Lilly... had [a] smile of enlightenment.... At that moment Schnabel stopped and said, "And now you play."
She played the piece with far less competent technique
than before, far more like the child she was, more
naively—but convincingly.... Schnabel turned to me
and said, "Do you hear it? That's good. As long as you
play what you hear, that's music."[12]

Schnabel was a brilliant learning tactician: he combined the
skills of wisdom to trigger a profound insight in that student and
that situation. Note that Schnabel first *catalyzed* the situation by
challenging her, in fact by provoking her when he said she was
faking. Then he *showed* her what he wanted her to do. Then he *accompanied* her progression. Thus, the sequence used by Schnabel in
his music lesson was *catalyze → show → accompany*. His style was
particularly provocative; another maestro may have used a different combination or even different skills. That Schnabel was able to
create enlightenment in his student is the result of his ability to see
what she needed, as well as the ability to master the skills he used.

In short, the skills offered here do not constitute a recipe that,
if mindlessly followed, produces learning. Rather, they are useful in-
gredients that must be selected, refined, and mixed according to the
situation and resources available.

What really anchors these skills is the correspondence between
the way managers develop people in today's organizations and the
great learning systems of the past. The earlier schools of wisdom
were often geared for adults. Such is the case with the Socratic
method, for example, which is a *harvesting* strategy. Although invented more than 2,000 years ago, it is the very backbone of the

case study method used in today's business schools. Likewise, the wisdom of accompaniment draws from the education developed by craftspeople in the Middle Ages; the wisdom of sowing harkens back to the education favored by religions born in the Middle East; the wisdom of the catalyst finds its sources in shamanism and heroism. The essence of each of these five skills is grounded in the correspondence between a well-developed historical example and a major contemporary managerial practice in a given successful organization somewhere in the world.

. . . .

The Career as Personal Development

Classical management systems had to provide a "ladder of development" for employees to climb. This model was the basis for career development in the expansion years following World War II. Individual progress within an organization was marked by promotion stages, title changes, and corresponding rises in salary. Individual development was identified with moving up the ladder and proceeded according to effort, potential, and ability to handle responsibility. The ladder itself rested on a moral contract binding the individual and the institution through mutual interdependency. The elements of the classical social contract of management were job security, promotion, and training.

For the exceptional worker, there was always the opportunity to leap from blue to white collar—all the way to the top in some cases. The opportunity to move up was considered a democratic form of justice.

Learning New Rules for New Times

Employment has become an entrepreneurial undertaking even for the average worker, who must now maintain work and develop him- or herself inside an organization. The rules of the game have changed. Job security, promotion, and training have been replaced by job insecurity, personal responsibility for career growth, and an open market for skills.

Even in Europe, where there was considerable resistance to the so-called American insensitivity to workers' need of security, the 1990s have brought about the same shifts. And in Japan, where a career was once seen as a lifelong fealty to one employer, the shift has also begun. For the large Japanese company, preserving lifelong employment gave each worker a place in society, which was more important than applying Western management tools for extracting short-term performance from individuals. But the message now heard in Japan is, "Farewell to the devoted workaholic manager and welcome to managers who are able to work with non-Japanese and who have some measure of individuality."[1]

Psychologist Takeo Doi writes, "People's sense of belonging has faded and...their sense of social roles has become extremely fluid. Young people...can no longer grasp their identities. Even adults who once thought they knew themselves very well are now often placed in situations where they must ask themselves again just who they are. In this way the word *identity* has become indispensable for expressing the consciousness of contemporary mankind."[2]

Thus, the notion that the individual is ultimately responsible for his or her career is becoming a reality throughout developed economies. This move to individual responsibility underscores the need to ask essential questions of life and define one's role in society—a process inseparable from wisdom.

A new model of employee development is becoming the norm in many organizations. The Career Action Center in Palo Alto, California, a nonprofit, career-management group, is supported by individual members and corporate clients like Apple Computer, Sun Microsystems, Raychem Corporation, and other Silicon Valley firms. Increasingly, says Program Director Betsy Collard, "People see the need to keep their skills current and are taking responsibility for their own careers."[3]

Raychem, for instance, has created an in-house career center to help people manage their own professional development and pursue opportunities within the 11,000-employee company. Stephen Balogh, former general manager of a $100 million Raychem unit who became vice president of human resources in 1990, says the "soft sciences" of employee development and organizational learning are now as critical as technical expertise:

> We've learned that even brilliant patents and global location strategies can be imitated. So we've turned to the human frontier and tried to celebrate the value that our people and our organizational design bring to us. Coming into an HR position—which like most corporate functions is usually under attack as a drain on resources—I tried to figure out how to add value. What came to me was the idea of championing a culture where employees understood that it is as much their responsibility as their managers' to develop their careers, and it is their managers' responsibility to attract and develop talent.... It's the leaders' job to show managers that there's no distinction between learning and working. They are one and the same.[4]

In short, the rules of the game have changed, and they go something like this: *Your career depends on you, and you had better work at increasing your own long-term value, because nobody is going to do it for you.* Employers, in turn, have accepted this reality: *In the new marketplace for talent, we must provide opportunities, resources, and rewards for the continual development of our workforce or risk losing our greatest competitive asset.*

Setting a Value on Learning at Work

The new work contract creates a benchmark for the value of managers in enhancing work, by telling employees *the company cannot guarantee you lifetime employment, but you will progress with the assistance of excellent managers. This is much more than just a job, it is a bridge to future employability.*

With changing roles and responsibilities at work, we are likely to see individuals paying in some form or another for the learning organizations now provide. Learning contracts have been studied extensively by adult educators, particularly Malcolm Knowles.[5] Learning contracts can be formalized by monetary payment for which a negotiated percentage of salary would be invested, or with learning loans on the model of today's student loans, possibly financed through flexible-benefit and retirement funds.

Thus, people may find themselves having to invest not just their own time and effort, but also their own money to enhance their careers. If this happens, employee attitudes toward training are likely to change. A recent British study shows what happens when people faced the prospect of paying for their own training. Of 311 managers surveyed who had left their companies because of redundancy and become freelance workers, fewer than 25 percent took training courses. When asked why, they said when they looked at training programs in terms of value for money, they found the market rampant with "gross overpricing and indifferent quality."[6]

One answer to the question of who pays (and how) comes from Swissôtel, an international subsidiary of Swissair. Heinrich Grafe, general manager of Swissôtel's Beijing property, faced a growing need for capable managers—and a largely unskilled staff. With the boom of new hotels in Beijing, a skilled worker or manager could easily leave a job and get a 50 percent raise elsewhere. Why be loyal at such a price?

As a result, many hotel managers provided minimal training of Chinese workers, because they knew they'd likely lose their investment. But Swissôtel was obliged to develop local Chinese in their joint-venture contract, and the Chinese owners were insistent on developing people. So Grafe invented a payback contract for learning. He sent prospective managers abroad to other hotels for training, and in return asked them to make a three-year commitment to stay in the company. Any employee attending a long-term certified training course was asked to commit for at least the duration of the training program, usually about two years. Employees could leave any time, but if they did, they or their future employer would have to reimburse Swissôtel for its training investment.

Such deals are not just limited to the transfer of knowledge in developing countries. Germany's apprenticeship programs also formalize employees' commitment to employers in return for career development. And in the United States, some organizations that make educational loans to employees now offer to forgive those debts if employees agree to stay with the company.

Becoming a Mentor

Taking responsibility for the personal and professional development of others means we are expected to create the basis for individual success.

The word *mentor* is mythological in origin, the name of a friend of Ulysses, hero of *The Odyssey*. An old and wise man to whom the warrior entrusts his son when he sets out on the war against the Trojans. Mentor is above all a guardian, and he keeps watch not only over the son but also of Odysseus' household. In the story, Mentor helps the young man find his father and at times incarnates Athena, the goddess of wisdom, to advise the young man.

To become a mentor now requires a minimal understanding of psychological development. What do we know of personal development today?

Early in the twentieth century, Swiss psychologist Carl Gustav Jung, a dissident psychoanalyst who eventually left his mentor Sigmund Freud, attempted to understand the development of the healthy individual. Jung described the level at which a person reaches true adult maturity as "individuation"—that is, a state attained when one is able to master the social demands of work and raising a family and balance them with the unconscious desires and dreams we all have about what we would like to be.[7]

Following Jung's insight, social psychologist Erik Erikson described a state he called "generativity,"[8] an attitude of caring for others and a decision to help others benefit from one's own knowledge and experience. Erikson emphasized an important point: concern for others as a mature adult brings with it an increase in one's own creativity and resourcefulness. Refusal to shift focus from self to others, according to Erikson, is often accompanied by failure at this stage of life and shows an inadequacy in assuming responsibility.

This early work of psychologists eventually led to study of personal development as a social phenomenon. In the late 1970s, Harvard sociologist Daniel Levinson mapped the adult life stages of American men.[9] A few years later, Gail Sheehy awakened Americans to the idea of "passages" with her best-seller of that title. Sheehy provided lively characterizations of the diverse experiences people have when shifting from one stage of life to another. She also underscored the differences between women's and men's life stages. Like Jung and Erikson, sociologists emphasized reaching midlife is, in fact, a positive stage of maturity—the plenitude of active life—as in this assessment by Sheehy: "For those who face this major passage and make peace with themselves, the mid-forties can bring a strengthened sense of self and a refreshed sense of purpose, ushering in a stage of renewal in the fifties that can be a gateway to life's most confident and satisfying years."[10]

Unfortunately, corporate human resource managers have largely ignored the work of these psychologists and sociologists. Midlife was seen as a dangerous stage in a career where a person's skills were no longer up to date and one's contribution became of questionable use to the company. Those who reach midlife still may find themselves wondering if they can really make it if they are thrown into the job market; as a consequence, they try to hang on until retirement—not a very promising situation for undertaking what, according to Sheehy, should be our most "confident and satisfying years." Women find themselves penalized in career development by being forced onto a "mommy track," even though taking time off to raise children is a vital activity for any society. And if workers ever want to take time off work to "find themselves," try an alternative life-style, or define new long-term goals—again a normal passage in an adult's development—they are labeled unstable. The entire value system of the corporate career is insensitive to the realities of how people develop, and it ignores that passing from one stage to the next provides the most valuable resources for learning.

Learning leaders, mentors, and managers must set aside these outmoded career notions and focus on the personal and professional needs of those they hope to develop. They must understand how these needs may change according to the growth of the learner and must identify and leverage personal learning passages.

At the risk of oversimplification, we focus on two stages of learning development: apprenticeship, where one first engages in new learning, and championship, where one begins to master the work at hand. Individuals go through these stages more than once as they advance in their careers. Learning to learn, like learning languages, is something people get better at the more they do it.

Managing Apprenticeship

An apprentice has frequent contact with a coach to learn the tricks of the trade. One often seeks the further guidance of a mentor, a senior figure in the organization who is not the apprentice's direct manager. In terms of learning, one brings to apprenticeship an intellectual culture of knowledge, complete with references (what constitutes valid knowledge), attitudes (which define one's relationship to learning), and languages (for research measurement, interpretation, and expression). Here, the cultural capital one accumulates is learned in a very different way from school. It will take years to master.

Before entering into apprenticeship, the individual should have acquired some mastery of self-learning or learning to learn.

For many, apprenticeship can be a frustrating experience because it carries little responsibility. Coaches and mentors must, therefore, make learning interesting and rich. Apprentices also need role models—mere technical training will not do. Vertical relationships are needed, but they have to be based on the learning relationship rather than on authority.

Managing Championship

A different form of learning comes when one gains responsibility for projects and people. The individual focuses on action; trial and error are essential. One can only learn effectively at this stage if the management system allows risk-taking and innovation.

Champions in a dynamic organization are difficult to manage: they can be impatient and proud and tend not to see their own mistakes objectively. On the other hand, they are motivated (and can often be manipulated) by charismatic leaders who know how to lure, stroke, and reward them.

In terms of learning, champions often focus on the quick fix and the directly useful with a what's-in-it-for-me attitude. Paradoxically, however, champions tend to be concerned about ethical problems and have strong ideals. They are often on a quest for personal meaning as a counterpoint to their focus on results at work.

Learning for survival, the renewal of wisdom, and the reinvention of careers are three facets of a revolution sweeping the workplace. Yet in most organizations, even as the need for learning grows, valuable learning resources are left fallow.

The following table outlines how the five skills of wisdom apply to apprenticeship and championship. In the chapters that follow, we will show how successful learning organizations have capitalized on the wisdom of managers to develop their employees.

Table 3.1. Applying the Skills of Wisdom to Adult Learning.

	Apprentice	Champion
Accompany	Professions such as medicine, law, and journalism offer internship programs. Japanese companies provide entry-level workers with a dedicated supervisor and long-term programs for integration into a lifelong career. German apprenticeship programs provide Meisters. U.S. trade unions have a system of apprentice, journeyman, and master worker.	In professions such as consulting, banking, and law, champions are supervised by an older partner. In sales organizations, regional sales managers usually spend about 50 percent of their time coaching, often systematically through mentoring programs.
Sow	In-house employee orientation programs usually sow the seeds of the corporate culture.	Leaders often sow subliminal messages in the minds of champions to impart a vision of the future and to inspire action.
Catalyze	Most apprenticeship programs do not explicitly address this dimension. Job rotation and working internationally provide some experience.	Champions are often the object of catalytic situations involving performance and responsibility. Taking responsibility for a team or a department is a well-known catalytic experience. Giving challenging objectives often catalyzes performance.

Table 3.1. Applying the Skills of Wisdom to Adult Learning, Cont'd.

	Apprentice	Champion
Show	Coaches, masters, and mentors set an example for imitation as they show how to perform a task or execute a procedure.	Leaders, especially charismatic leaders, draw on the power of showing conviction and commitment as a tool of influence. Networks allow people to interact and to develop demonstrative knowledge. Participation in team situations provides a forum for exchange and socialization where people learn to show or reveal themselves.
Harvest	Harvesting usually requires moving to the next stage, where the apprentice takes charge and performs at a higher level. Some action-training programs put value on what is produced during apprenticeship. Many industries benefit by employing young people as apprentices.	Good managers responsible for champions are expert at spurring initiative. Some organizations generate innovations and new projects systematically.

Part II

. . . .

The Timeless Skills of Wisdom

4

Accompanying

The word *accompany* is related to *companion*: both come from the Latin *com* and *panis* meaning to break bread with. This is also the origin of the word *company*.

The idea of a journey is implied in accompaniment. One becomes a companion by traveling the same road and sharing one's bread with others. We will see how the French word *compagnon* designates a type of learning that was widespread throughout Europe from the eleventh to the fourteenth centuries and lives on even today in some management systems.

In Asia, accompaniment is an extraordinarily important word because it refers to learning as a way; the Chinese *tao* or Japanese *do* is perhaps the most fundamental word in Oriental philosophy. It is found not only in Taoist writings but also in Confucianist and Buddhist texts. Any learning of a skill involving self-improvement, whether it be flower arrangement, martial arts, or calligraphy, is called a way. The meaning of master in Oriental philosophy is closely related to accompaniment in these *tao*. Taking the road as a learning journey, whether it be a simple field trip or a quest or a pilgrimage, is practically universal: we find it in the journey to Mecca in Islam and in the medieval romantic notion of the knightly quest.

Learning as a journey is a powerful image, embedded in archaic Western mythology and language. The words *career* and *coach* derive from this metaphor; the former comes from the French *carrière*, meaning a track for racing horses, and the latter from the French *coche*, meaning a chariot or wagon. By extension, *coach* is used not only for the vehicle but also for the driver who guides it. In India, one of the most celebrated classics is the *Bhagavad Gita*; it recounts how the warrior Arjuna receives guidance on the meaning of life from his chariot driver, Krishna, god of the True Way. Homer's *Iliad* has a similar story of the warrior Achilles who loses his companion in battle and finds another driver, Automedon, whose name means he who thinks by himself. And Plato's famous metaphor of the chariot as the soul in the *Phaedrus* has had profound influence on the Western concept of the mind.

Every manager concerned with wisdom knows it is often necessary to make the journey with the learner. To accompany is, first and foremost, to be present and attentive; this can actually be more important than actively intervening in learning. To the extent that the management of a company encourages learning, it needs companions, coaches, mentors, and guides. Accompanying, more than any other learning skill, justifies the learning manager's presence within the organization.

There are, of course, cases when accompaniment is not available—for instance, in start-up companies, where the coaches and guides tend to be outsiders rather than managers—or even desirable, as in creative organizations such as ad agencies, media companies, or research laboratories, where the presence of manager types can be an irritation.

Accompaniment has always been important in human development, as any parent can attest; the growth of what we call the professions is proof that skilled accompaniment meets a basic human need. Doctors accompany patients, lawyers accompany clients, consultants accompany companies. . . . Today, there are professions for accompanying pregnant women, drug addicts, hyperactive children, compulsive gamblers, fat people, lonely people, poor people, and the dying.

A Journey Behind Bars

One of the most visionary accompanists we know is Dennis Luther, who has been the warden of the Federal Correctional Institution McKean. McKean is the top-rated prison in the United States for safety of staff and inmates and for overall quality of living and working conditions. The medium-security prison houses 1,400 inmates, many of them hardened criminals who have spent most of their adult lives behind bars. Most of the 350 corrections officers and staff are tough careerists who during the years have literally banged heads with the worst inmates the prison system has to offer. In short, McKean is no country club, and there are no coddlers on staff.

But in a setting where pure command-and-control management is still an option, Luther has fostered trust, ethics, and enlightened self-interest to guide the institution. He focuses on people's deeper need for the basic respect usually denied inmates and staff. The warden makes clear he has seen the worst and best humanity has to offer; his constituents know that, like themselves, he has truly "been there."

Luther gives his staff and inmates a role in running the institution. Accompaniment for Luther means daily meetings with staff and strolls through the inmate cafeteria. He is accessible to anyone with a problem or question. He takes the pulse of the inmate population through regular surveys and allows the inmates to actively participate in a wide range of clubs and organizations that raise money for prison activities and local charities. Accompaniment is also communal: the clubs and charitable activities serve as self-directed peer learning groups. The staff, in turn, accompany in self-managed teams that cut through the traditional chain of command and, under the guidance of Luther's Leadership Team, take on quality improvement and operational, staff development, or special projects.

Luther's management by accompaniment has changed the dynamic of prison life from a climate of fear and intimidation to an ethic of mutual respect and personal growth. Since opening in 1990, the prison has had no escapes, murders, serious assaults, sexual assaults, or suicides. Posted throughout the facility is Luther's list of twenty-eight beliefs about the treatment of inmates. Among them:

- Correctional workers have a *responsibility* to ensure that inmates are returned to the community no more angry or hostile than when they were committed.

- Whenever possible, staff must *provide explanations* for changes in policies and procedures that inmates perceive as detracting from the quality of life.

- There is inherent value in self-improvement programs, such as education, whether or not these programs are related to recidivism.

- Some inmates are very intelligent or knowledgeable. Don't be threatened, but instead capitalize on their skills.

Luther's brilliance as a manager is to create a setting where such values can thrive, even under difficult circumstances. He considers the development of professional talent an explicit goal and has recruited the best and the brightest from the Bureau of Prisons to work at McKean.

Accompaniment also means letting learning happen. Luther makes clear to new inmates that their behavior will determine how they are treated during their stay. Likewise, his message to staff is different from what they might expect: "There is nothing you can do, no mistake you can make, that's going to cost you anything. We might talk about it, there might be some counseling or strong words; but once I've decided you are worth the investment of mentoring and developing, there is no punishment for failing."[1]

In the charged prison atmosphere, staff members encounter

daily, even hourly, challenges, each of which Luther considers a learning opportunity. Besides intense encounters with inmates and other staff (who work largely in self-directed teams responsible for much of their own decision making), Luther has devised an effective tool for accompanying learning: he hands a selected manager an unfamiliar, sometimes unwanted, assignment. "I very consciously put people through some exercises to see if they have the right stuff," says Luther. "I like to assign people projects they may not be comfortable with, tasks to test what their growth potentials are and to help develop strategies to overcome their limitations. I can pick up a lot about their values, their intelligence, their inclination to accept risks."

Luther evinces a profound loyalty and respect from staff and inmates alike. For inmates, it's largely a matter of returning the respect Luther shows them in an environment where personal honor is everything. Associate Warden Craig Apker speaks for many staff members:

> Dennis Luther seems to focus most on the development of those skills that are personally enriching and have the effect of enhancing one's quality of life. Looking to the warden as a mentor, I find nearly every lesson is in what I value, what's right, or how we humans interact with others. What I do with these lessons guides how I decide to contribute to the orderly operation of the institution.... The impact is first and foremost personal.... I have also experienced Warden Luther's commitment to working on his own development. This serves as an example that encourages people to develop their strengths and seize the opportunities offered.... In other words, nobody develops as much as the person who is trying to help others develop.[2]

McKean offers a raft of formal training programs, from physical conditioning to customer service and leadership development. In staff surveys, McKean management received an 83 percent favorable rating for its support of training (versus 71 percent for the Bureau of Prisons overall); and the training itself was considered effective by 80 percent of those surveyed (versus 65 percent for the bureau overall). But beyond classroom training, Luther's achievement has been to set a tone. In daily staff meetings where problems are frankly and collegially discussed and in one-on-one dealings with his managers, Luther makes clear his expectations and shares the wisdom of his twenty-two-year career. More than any of the five learning skills, accompanying is advanced through personal presence, supportive attitude, and faith in the human capacity for growth and change.

The McKean experience teaches us that:

- Anybody, even prison inmates, can respond to accompaniment over time—with dramatic results.

- Accompaniment as a form of leadership requires trust and accessibility.

- As in any organization, the key to success is a commitment by middle managers to accompany development rather than try to exert personal power.

- Accompaniment demands programs in which people can participate in learning, seek training, and marshal learning resources.

Companies, Fellowships, and Brotherhoods

In Europe during the late Middle Ages and until the beginning of the Industrial Revolution, accompaniment was an innovative force in the confluence of work and learning. The system that preceded it was the guild system or "corporation" in which professional status was attributed only to those who followed an apprenticeship.

Workers, whether they were bakers, bricklayers, or buttonmakers, didn't go to school; they worked with a master and learned by doing. It was not enough, however, to be an able and determined apprentice to become a master; more important was having the money to start a shop and having been born into one of the families comprising the guild or corporation.

Starting in the eleventh century, young workers began revolting against this system by taking to the road and escaping the control of the corporations. They would work a bit here and a bit there, improving their skill by going from one site to the other. This was, of course, illegal. Consequently, the networks of young worker-companions were underground "companies." Companions were able to recognize one another by nicknames, passwords, hand signals, and so on, and there were initiation ceremonies for new members. At each building site, company members would try to contact a fellow companion hoping to be lodged in his house—the host companion's wife, the "mother," was a major figure in the system and the subject of admiration, as well as many ribald jokes and songs. As progression in skill was related to the quality of the work, the great sites—especially cathedrals—attracted these self-liberated apprentices like magnets.

This phenomenon of companies, fellowships, and brotherhoods became extremely significant for the history of Europe during the next five centuries and beyond. Some networks of skilled workers became secret societies and formed their own beliefs, often at odds with church doctrine. Already in the twelfth century, the Vaudois community, founded in Lyon by Pierre Vaudès, taught that all Christians should study Holy Scriptures, there should be no special status for the clergy, and ministers should be workers and itinerant teachers. The Vaudois, even though condemned as heretics, spread to England, Flanders, Germany, Bavaria, Bohemia, Poland, Austria, Hungary, and Italy.

A similar group, the Brotherhood of Bohemia, laid the foundations for a school system where children studied religion; learned to read, write, count, and sing; practiced physical exercise; and learned a skilled trade. By the fifteenth century, the company concept had become the model for the Protestant organizations inspired by Luther and Calvin. Many of the esoteric secret societies of today, notably the Freemasons and the Rosicrucians, were originally created as companies for the education of workers. The goal of this accompaniment type of learning is succinctly defined by Jean Bernard, one of the principal proponents of the French *compagnonnage* system after World War I: "It is all about the personal realization of the skilled tradesman—especially the manual worker in the building trades—in order to guide him to knowledge by starting with his hands and working up to his spirit in order to increase his breadth of being."[3]

The dignity of the skilled worker and identification with a trade via the company have an influence on manual labor in Europe even today, though its importance was severely diminished when U.S. management style was imported after World War II. In France before the war, you could find some 200,000 *compagnons* on the road for the traditional Tour de France, working and learning at the important building sites. Today, we think of the Tour de France only as a bicycle race.

A contemporary example of a learning strategy based on accompaniment is Grenoble's program for entrepreneurs. Daniel Panel, a professor of economics, was dissatisfied with the knowledge resources available to people who want to launch a business; what they got was information about administrative requirements and how to write a business plan. Panel thought the essential element to help would-be entrepreneurs get started—personal contact with other entrepreneurs—was missing. A simple workshop or lecture series would not do; it had to be a process of osmosis where entrepreneurship would be transferred over time in a natural relationship. So Panel established the Centre d'Application à la Fonction Entrepreneuriale de Rhône Alpes (CAFERA) with a group of local entrepreneurs who mentored the candidates for six weeks.

The participants shadowed these entrepreneurs, asked them questions, and scrutinized their companies. The candidates kept a journal and filled out questions in a booklet designed by Panel. Every week, they had feedback sessions with other candidates, Panel, or a colleague as facilitator. At the end of the accompaniment process, the candidates spent a week at a mountain retreat to formulate their project and present it to a jury formed by the mentor-entrepreneurs who participated in CAFERA. This experiment uncovered three important facts of accompaniment:

1. The candidates were able to more effectively learn what they needed to know (and at much less cost!) in free interaction with entrepreneurs than if they had spent all their time in a classroom.

2. Many mentor-entrepreneurs simply did not know how to accompany people; they lacked the necessary patience, openness, and capacity for companionship in an unstructured context.

3. Those entrepreneurs who were good natural mentors wanted to improve their skills with some basic knowledge of psychology and accompaniment; thus, CAFERA had to set up a seminar for the mentors to discuss the skills of accompaniment.

Psychology of Accompaniment

The history of accompaniment in Europe received another, and quite surprising, impetus from an undercurrent that may well have remained marginal had it not been for Sigmund Freud. Thanks to his invention of psychotherapy, in which he built on the work of the hypnotists, a new form of accompaniment, therapy, was born — a true innovation.

This is not to say that managers should become therapists. Psychotherapy is not management. What is relevant is not the theory or even the practice of psychotherapy; it is the contribution Freud made to the concept of an effective learning relationship, particularly the notion of transfer.

Thanks to Freud we know a relationship in which one person helps another harbors a powerful subconscious process and is fraught with pitfalls. In the mentoring relationship, limits are needed and distance must be maintained; it is too easy for people who help others to abuse the relationship. We may know nothing at all about psychotherapy, but we all need to know something about transfer.

Transfer is one of the two pillars of Freud's theory of the unconscious. (The other is the concept of repression, in which painful memories, wishes, and desires are "pushed down" into unconsciousness.) In transfer, the behavior characteristic of one relationship, usually the primary relationship between a child and a parent, is transferred to other relationships. In the relationship of accompaniment, there is a positive attraction of one for the other. Freud discovered, however, this positive transfer is followed during accompaniment by a negative transfer as the patient or learner becomes more autonomous, and the therapist is rejected. This is actually a sign of progress, and Freud emphasized that neither positive nor negative transfer is to be considered a mature and balanced judgment of the therapist in the relationship.

Transfer is thus a process that has to be well managed, and it is up to the accompanist not to confuse issues in the process. Freud, of course, was excessively concerned that the therapist who was exploring powerful desires and memories with the patient should maintain distance. Sitting behind the patient who would be free-associating while lying on a couch was part of his precautionary technique. Another was that one should only listen, grunt from time to time, and take notes—but never tell the patient what one was writing!

In accompaniment, we see the parting of the ways between management and therapy. The needs, the goals, and the relationships are not the same; it would be naive to expect that the techniques of one should be valid for the other. On the other hand, it is clear Freud had discovered something important in the dynamics of accompaniment. Mentors should not see themselves through the eyes of the learner; it is a projected image that will probably end in rejection.

The discussion of transfer offers the following lessons:

- Although it can be personally revealing, accompaniment is a professional relationship that can become dangerous to the learner if confused with deep friendship or romance.

- The learner projects images on the mentor that change according to the dynamics of the learning process.

- Managerial accompaniment is not therapy; the mentor and learner have a collegial relationship marked by shared experience and the practical realities of work.

The mentor must know how to manage distance and recognize warning signals. And yet the managed relationship must be natural and spontaneous. Ultimately, accompaniment constitutes the heart of business dealings. We were struck by the story of one consultant who described his professional growth in stages—from a tentative, ill-at-ease rookie to a cocky overachiever to a committed companion. He recalls:

> I was working with a client, but was reluctant to share all my expertise; I felt I knew more than he did, and, frankly, I felt I should have his job. Then one day he looked me in the eye and said, "Can you help me? I am quite lost." There was no false modesty, no dramatization; in one sentence, all the cards were on the table. At that moment, I had the impression that I understood

what was noble about business and heard myself say, "So that's what it's all about!" There was no more client and no consultant; just two men who would walk the same path and build something together. I accepted the commitment. Since that meeting, whatever my interest for the company or for the project in question, I intuitively weigh my engagement in terms of who I am to accompany. If there is no potential for friendship in the relationship, I let the project go. This may not be the most efficient way of selling consulting services, but it has become of capital importance for me in my work.

Companions of Minorange

The world's largest construction company, established by Francis Bouygues in 1952, is an excellent example of how a traditional form of wisdom has been revived in a modern management concept.

At the time, there was a boom in the construction industry due to the rebuilding of Europe after World War II. This business had changed significantly because of the improvements in managing construction projects and the use of new building materials and methods. Bouygues was at the forefront of these developments in France. Yet, he was also keenly aware that the success of a builder depended on working methods and what he called the "spirit" of work. The problem was that there were not enough French builders to do the work. Before the war, French workers comprised 80 percent of all construction workers in France; after the war, their numbers had dropped to 50 percent and today they represent only 20 percent.

So Bouygues, like other builders, recruited Belgians, Italians, Portuguese, and Yugoslavs. But it was still not enough. The army of workers in France came mostly from North Africa, especially Algeria, just as in Germany workers came from Turkey. And the monstrous rabbit-hutch apartment buildings hastily constructed outside the capital cities of Europe are their horrendous monuments. But at least those who had once lived in shantytowns could enjoy the relative luxury of low-rent apartments with running water, central heating, and indoor toilets.

The problem in these boom years was that as soon as workers acquired a small measure of skill, competitors would hire them away. Bouygues found himself in 1962 with a turnover rate of 180 percent![4] Then he got an idea. He had always had high esteem for the *compagnon* movement, even though he was highly educated, with an engineering degree from the prestigious Ecole Centrale. What he would do, he decided, would be to reinvent the European tradition of accompaniment.

Here, Bouygues showed a deep insight into the motivation of the immigrant worker. An Italian worker in France was looked down upon; an Algerian was often openly ostracized. What meant more than money to these workers was respect and responsibility, a place in society. So Bouygues created the first modern company of construction workers, using the name of a fast-drying paint, minium orange; thus, the Order of the Companions of Minorange was born. In fact, Bouygues killed two birds with one stone: he solved his problem of bringing workers quickly up to speed on the building sites without expensive training courses and kept his best and most skilled workers by naming them companions. Only companions could wear the green uniform; the others wore blue. Only companions would do a Tour de France. Only companions could wear stars on their hard hats, one star for each of three levels: novice, first degree, and second degree.

Each year, Bouygues convened his companions for a celebration he personally planned and attended. He could count on his master workers, mostly foreigners who found in Bouygues a leader who trusted and respected them. By 1966, the turnover rate for companions at Bouygues's company was only 2 percent. Today, Bouygues is a market leader, directing construction projects throughout the world. Bouygues now has many Orders of Companions, but they all follow the same general rules as the original Order of Minorange: the brotherhoods are composed only of skilled workers with two years' experience; they are nominated by their managers; and if they themselves are promoted to a supervisory position, they must leave the order.

What most strongly characterizes the revival of this medieval system by Bouygues is that he has preserved strong ethical criteria for fellowship. A companion is assessed by his peers in terms such as team spirit, setting an example for others, sense of discipline, and morality. These words simply are not used in typical performance reviews, and Bouygues's appraisal forms for managers do not focus on them.

In the future, the *compagnon* system at Bouygues will probably spread to management levels and become more professional. The company's strategy is to invest heavily in Asia and Eastern Europe: what worked when Bouygues's management was French will now have to become more international. Also, the company will have to become professional in the international transfer of its know-how. Already, Michel Bétant, deputy general manager of Bouygues's International Building-Asia branch, is beginning to use accompaniment as a management system for the transfer of know-how to Asian engineers and project managers.[5] Although this involves the challenge of bridging the culture gap, there is every reason to believe the wisdom that was successful for 800 years of European *compagnonnage* can be modernized and explained cross-culturally.

The Bouygues example suggests the following lessons on how to manage accompaniment on a mass scale:

- Culture is important. The Bouygues *compagnons* felt themselves an extension of a centuries-old tradition.

- Motivation is key. For Bouygues, the goal for the learner in the accompaniment process was recognition and participation, especially for foreign workers or outsiders.

- Shared values underpin the accompaniment process.
  The minorange companions are accepted into the
  order only if they uphold its values, and they are assessed on these points by their peers.

Accompanists as Storytellers

The best news about accompanying learning is that most of us already do it—in friendship, parenting, or helping others. As Luther
has shown, the essential requirement is a genuine belief in "the inherent value of self-improvement." As Bouygues has shown, you
have to tap into the fundamental motivation of workers if you want
them to buy in.

Another manager, working in a far different context, provides a
further example. Diana Edwards is a management training consultant and former director of organizational development at San
Francisco's four-star Pan Pacific Hotel. As we'll see in Chapter
Seven, she uses the "wisdom and personal judgment of front-line
people" to spur learning and change. Before entering the business
world, Edwards spent a year-and-a-half as a missionary in South
America, where she helped women in remote villages organize economic, social, and health-improvement projects—a process she
describes as "accompanying" the villagers in their daily lives. Edwards says her most important insights came from her grandfather,
who ran a family ice business in Oakland, California.

> Mostly what I know about that ice business is the stories
> my grandfather told about the people who worked for
> him. He knew all the drivers, their troubles, when they
> got married, had babies. That was the value of the busi-
> ness to him. I tell his story to a lot of people at work. . . .
> I tell people in training seminars, forget about the P&L
> statement for a minute. Work on yourselves. Be better
> people. If I were general manager of a hotel I'd ask all the

departments to tell me their people's stories....Good management is not about parachuting in and patting people on the back. It's about hanging out, being available, sharing stories. It's about real involvement with the people you work with.[6]

Edwards is personally and emotionally accessible to those she is responsible for training; she counsels managers to do likewise—by spending time with front-line workers, understanding their concerns, sharing stories, and demonstrating their values. It is personal commitment that will set the stage for the changes every organization faces.

Accompaniment is the ability to travel the road of learning with another. Learning leaders, managers, and mentors who ask how to accompany wisdom should consider the actions we've described in Chapter Four.

- Make the commitment to travel the same road as the learner and to share your experiences in mutual dialogue.

- Be available to others, continually spell out your message, give clear support and expectations to managers, and provide resources that enable others to turn goals into reality.

- Acknowledge the dignity of work and recognize the need for workers to organize their own learning efforts.

- Provide training to mentors in the fundamentals of psychology and the pitfalls inherent in the transfer relationship.

- Hang out, share stories, and show you care.

5

. . . .

Sowing

Sowing intellectual seeds is a metaphor from the time when land began to be cultivated in Mesopotamia—when nomads first settled in one place, developed cities, created government, and invented writing. The relationship between cultivating the mind and cultivating the earth is strong and deep; there are many parallels between farming and education—for example, the seed must be good and the soil suitable. Or the parallel of the seasons for planting and reaping. We find the metaphor of sowing in many cultures, of course; but in the Mediterranean basin, the metaphor of the seed is particularly important for Judaism, Christianity, and Islam. All three religions use the same metaphors: the seed represents the divine word, the earth is like the spirit of man, and the Book serves to cultivate the spirit so the seed can take root and flourish.

These religions hold that spiritual awakening is the direct result of the word of God spoken through a patriarch, a prophet, or a master. Each preaches the supremacy of its message above all others. The absolute conviction of believers may breed intolerance, however, as demonstrated by holy wars. The greatest danger of sowing is that once people are convinced of an absolute truth, they tend to eliminate, or at least convert, the nonbelievers.

The salient features of sowing, as distinct from accompaniment, are the mentor's intent to plant a message in the learner's mind and trust in the learner's ability to assimilate and understand the message when the time comes.

Sowing Skills

The exercise of sowing is not without pain or risk, as Bob Aubrey's personal experience makes clear:

> My most remarkable experience of sowing happened at a seminar I organized for an Indian medicine man, Swiftdeer, several years ago. As I was enthusiastic about his teachings, I decided to create the most memorable seminar possible. I rented a beautiful manor in the countryside outside Paris and invited many of my friends, as well as other teachers of shamanism and spirituality that I knew. There were also, of course, paying participants.
>
> The week was quite full, and there were a number of unforgettable moments: healing ceremonies, brilliant lecturing, an atmosphere of something special taking place. At the end, I felt the week had been extraordinary and was quite satisfied with myself. Although I knew I would never do it again, I was happy to have done it as a contribution—that is, until the concluding session of the seminar.
>
> There in the seminar room I found myself sitting beside Swiftdeer, and in front of me were fifty very angry, deeply disturbed faces. The tension in the room could be cut with a knife. The complaints started, and each was more critical than the last: "We didn't understand what Swiftdeer was teaching—he should have been clearer"; "You should have given us a seminar booklet so that we could follow"; "You didn't deliver on all the points mentioned in the announcement"; "We couldn't all be

in the healing ceremonies. You should have planned it so we could all participate equally"; "The invited guests didn't pay. Why should they have been given preference over us?" This went on for about an hour. Already tired from the week's work, I was totally deflated by these attacks. I felt like running out of the room. I wanted to cry.

But as I looked over to Swiftdeer sitting next to me, I couldn't believe his calm and poise. He took the criticism with grace, seemed interested in what they were saying and made sure everyone had a chance to speak his or her mind. My own mind was reeling. Maybe my seminar had been poorly organized after all. Having been a teacher before, surely I should have seen to it that everyone was following and that the important points were clearly spelled out and summarized.

I felt confused and bitter as the seminar participants, including my friends, filed out huffily. I turned to Swiftdeer, who seemed not to have minded the last hour at all: "How can you just take it?" I asked him dejectedly. He turned to me and said: "Bob, what happened just now was people letting out their energy. It means nothing. They got what they came for, but they think they didn't because they can't understand it yet. But I'll make you a bet: in a few months, they'll call you up and thank you for putting on this seminar." I replied: "Maybe we should have paid more attention to the teaching. They should have been able to understand what you were talking about." Swiftdeer chuckled: "Yeah, that's what teachers used to tell me. But I'll tell you a secret. I don't give a damn if people understand what I'm saying. I care even less about whether they like it or agree with me. What counts is that they have been moved; something changed inside them during this week, and all their complaints and criticisms are only a reaction to that unconscious change. I know what I'm doing." I was skeptical. But Swiftdeer won his bet. And I learned when one sows one must focus on the *intention* and not be affected by the reactions people have on receiving the message.

If you ask managers to be sowers, you are, at the outset, asking them to formulate what they know into a message. This commitment to wisdom is perhaps the most important aspect of sowing. A person who has no wisdom has, of course, nothing to sow. So the first step in sowing is the message, as the classic Sufi philosopher Jalaludin Rumi said: "You have a duty to perform. Do anything else, do any number of things, occupy your time fully, and yet, if you do not do this task, all your time will have been wasted."[1]

As we have seen, sowing is an art that requires time, patience, and observation. It also demands a profound respect for the nature of growth. As an art, sowing has little in common with an obsession for a quick return on investment and total control of outcomes. It also has little to do with what many teachers and students may consider good pedagogy. Sowing has its own dynamics.

Of course, it requires a certain humility. The CEO is rarely a prophet. The values of a corporate culture are not the Ten Commandments. The wisdom of the manager is not that of the Revelation. Some corporate cultures have a smug attitude of self-righteousness about them that gives them a dangerous taste for intolerance. They tend to recruit committed followers and mold them into the desired profiles; they reject anyone who dares question the corporate gospel or criticize the wisdom of its leaders. Such cultures can be quite dynamic and even spur high growth. But when it is time for a change, these cultures have to be restructured totally and tremendous resistance is encountered to giving up certitudes — even when they are patently outdated — in favor of openness, individual responsibility, and flexibility.

Sowing Success

Leon Royer, executive director of organizational learning for 3M, has developed a sowing strategy that has contributed tangibly to the company's success. A thirty-year company veteran, Royer had no traditional human resource management experience when he took over training for the $13 billion firm. He earned his stripes the way most people at 3M do—by building a record of technical and market achievement.

Royer has played a key role in developing two hit products—Scotchgard Carpet Protector and Post-it Notes. In typical 3M fashion, he was rotated throughout the company and asked to head new product start-ups. A relentlessly upbeat, energetic figure, Royer gives people the necessary tools and makes them responsible for their own success. Earlier in his career as a project manager, he had used every lost customer or other failure to prompt team problem-solving sessions; he used even routine production meetings as a learning forum to discuss product pricing, customer delight, and other business issues.

In selecting project-team members from the deep talent pools at 3M, Royer asked three questions:

1. What are you most proud of in your life?

2. What do you consider your greatest contribution to the profitable growth of the company?

3. Are you an enthusiastic person?

Royer says, "My job is removing obstacles and challenging people's imagination. I ask, 'How can I help you be the most productive, to continually grow as a person?'...I try to plant seeds, to create a winning attitude. It's a conscious part of what I do."[2]

A Society of Sowers

To see how another company manages sowing as a learning strategy, consider one founded in 1541. Ignatius of Loyola called it the Company or Society of Jesus, and it became the model of education based on the sowing of ideas. It still offers insights to the art of sowing in today's organizations.

This art was not invented by chance. Ignatius was responding to the changes during an extraordinary century for Europe. Erasmus expressed this best when he wrote: "Man is not born, he becomes." The roots of humanism were at the heart of the Jesuit project.

Throughout his life, Ignatius formulated and revised the fundamental inspiration of the Jesuit art of sowing, known as the Exercises. Their purpose was to allow adults to explore their will and to "fix" their way of life while preserving their individual liberty of choice. As a manual, a "guide for guides of the soul," the Exercises circulated among the members of the new society and was used in its missionary work.

The entire Jesuit system finds its power in the method of sowing ideas. For adults, the method involves the Exercises; but for college students, it is often called the Ratio Studorum, whose purpose is to sow the seeds of character that will allow them to make the right choices later in life. Jesuit organization recognizes clearly defined roles. There are three functions in Jesuit education:

1. The Prefect is the authority figure, in charge of giving orders and maintaining standards of excellence, like the headmaster in British schools.

2. The Director of Conscience is involved in personal dialogue with the individual and care of the soul. His role is to be open, to listen, to accompany.

3. The Regent (a function that has largely disappeared from Jesuit education) is a younger teacher or assistant responsible

for self-expression and character-building by organizing debates, plays, sports, and recreational activities.

Each function sows learning at a different level: one's rational mind, will, and social nature. In Jesuit practice, a mentor diagnoses a student's talent, counsels him or her in the choice of studies, guides the student concretely in those studies, and suggests necessary changes. A mentor also organizes the content of the pupil's studies, questions and introduces new ideas, and ensures the delivery of necessary teaching. Here, quite clearly, is a fully developed and truly effective concept of what it means to manage learning.

The Jesuit example contains valuable lessons for sowers in any organization.

- Structured activity—the Exercises—provides the context for sowing. The embedded message grows as the activity is repeated.

- Sowing is linked to a relationship. In the Jesuit system, these relationships are formal: the Prefect does not ask students to confide in him, and the Director of Conscience doesn't grade students. In work organizations, these roles may be informal, but different people are nevertheless associated with different messages.

- The Jesuit weakness, historically, has been its susceptibility to charges of manipulation of power. Unprincipled sowers can lead the organization to abuse its relationships with learners.

Humanizing While Downsizing

How does the manager's role change when a relationship of sowing learning replaces the traditional authoritarian relationship? What follows is the story of how Antoine Guichard, president of the

Casino Group, a 40,000-employee, international supermarket and distribution company based in France, tackled the problem. To fundamentally change the management culture of his company, Guichard showed himself to be a master of sowing techniques.

The Casino Group is nearly 100 years old, founded by Antoine's grandfather, Geoffroy Guichard, who established a chain of grocery stores in France in the late nineteenth century. Casino was the first company in France to turn the basic mom-and-pop grocery store into a chain, in 1898. After its initial expansion, the company grew little for fifty years. Then in the 1960s, Casino introduced the first supermarkets in France, based on the U.S. model. With this innovation, staffing levels in the company's headquarters exploded, and the white-collar echelons of finance, electronic data processing, human resources, and logistics began dictating objectives and directing store procedures.

This well-organized system made Casino number one in distribution in France until a new concept—hypermarkets three to five times the size of supermarkets—started competing. Without the managerial conditions necessary to adapt and innovate, the provincial company lagged behind its competitors. With the prospect of a single European market and the inevitable elimination of weak players, the future of Casino was clearly threatened. A deep and rapid change in Casino's managerial mentality was necessary.

At this point in 1989, Antoine Guichard became the unquestioned leader of Casino. He devised a two-pronged strategy. The first was international alliances with the British firm Argyll, owner of Safeway stores in the United Kingdom, and with Ahold in Holland, creating one of Europe's largest food-purchasing powers. The second was to sow the seeds of a new management culture through dialogue. Guichard knew he wouldn't see results right away, but he took the chance of transforming the company.

Guichard launched a corporate management institute to give his 2,000 managers a training ground. Then he reduced all management training to a single seminar entitled Change Management that all managers had to attend, and he made a commitment to personally explain his strategy to them. The operation hinged on Guichard's faith in his managers to take the seeds of autonomy into their hearts and abandon the previous authoritarian system. "The real question of the autonomy of people within a system is not answered by how many layers of hierarchy you have," says Guichard. "It is how people relate to each other. So what I did in my company was to change how people relate to each other within a hierarchy. I am trying to replace the traditional authority of the manager, which consists in ordering, controlling, and sanctioning, with three very different actions—listening, educating, and helping. That, I explain to my managers, is what they are henceforth paid to do."[3]

Sowing the seeds of a new management philosophy is for Guichard an operational management strategy. "When one sows seeds it takes time before one sees anything on the ground," he explains. "Have you ever noticed how long it seems when you seed a lawn? Then you wake up one morning to find a beautiful emerald carpet where yesterday there was only dirt! At Casino, our strategy is in place and I am in that anxious phase of waiting for shoots of the green carpet to push up through the ground."

It took five years for Guichard's strategy to pay off, and the effort looked shaky during the recession in Europe. But his patience eventually led Casino to a strong position in the highly competitive European market.

The Casino example offers the following lessons to those planning a sowing strategy:

- The message, if it concerns the whole company, has to come from the top and has to reflect the personal, genuine vision of the leader.

- Reducing management training to one seminar in a high-profile institute allowed the message to be clearly heard, even though many managers were unconvinced in the beginning.

- Patience in the face of adversity was Guichard's key
  strength. He knew it would take time for results to be
  visible, and this gave him courage to persevere.

Sowing Discomfort for Results

Bruce Jacobi is CEO of Intercounty Clearance Corporation, an
eighty-five-employee document-search service based in New York
City. ICC conducts public-records searches for banks, law firms,
and other businesses. It is exacting and unglamorous work; most
firms in the business provide little beyond basic, on-the-job training. But Jacobi, a training and development fanatic, sows the seeds
for constant skill-building, personal development, and professional
performance even before a new hire's first day on the job.

All job candidates are interviewed by a department manager,
the human resource manager, eight department employees (in
groups of two), and finally, Jacobi. The prerequisite for working at
ICC is the ability to learn, says Customer Service Manager Eric
Geringswald, who identifies that ability through such interview
questions as:

- What personal or business experiences have been most
  difficult, and what did you learn from them?

- How have you handled adversity?

- What are examples of important business or personal
  projects you have planned and how did they turn out?

For his part, Jacobi tries to prepare job candidates for what to
expect of him—and what he expects of them. "My job is to sell
them on ICC and tell them what they can expect if they choose to
work here," says Jacobi. "I explain that it's a flat organization, and
there are lots of opportunities to learn, but not a lot of fancy titles.
I tell them, 'If the things we expect of you make you nervous, that's

good. If you're going to be happy here, you have to be willing to live outside your comfort zone.'"[4]

Every manager is responsible for identifying and enhancing employees' skills. Both managers and front-line staff teach ICC University's sixteen-course curriculum, which includes software operation, personal communication, business law, and sales and marketing. Jacobi delivers leadership-development training to all employees, and every manager chooses appropriate learning exercises to include in departmental meetings. For example, before each meeting with his staff, Geringswald asks people to present a work-related topic—ways to improve the business, what they'd change in the operation, or pet peeves.

In addition, all customer service representatives—the people who conduct or coordinate most of the document searches for clients—receive formal sales training, with an emphasis on personal presentation. Why? At some point, says Geringswald, every employee is likely to be in front of a client. In fact, when problems arise, the customer service rep is expected to not only resolve the difficulty but also visit the client and explain what happened and how it was handled.

The demand that every employee learn new skills is supported by regular celebrations, personal encouragement, and tangible rewards. Part of every manager's job, says Geringswald, is to not only challenge employees to learn new skills but also to personally acknowledge and encourage their achievements. Once a year, ICC sponsors a companywide Appreciation Week, with certificates of achievements and other serious and frivolous awards presented to every employee who has completed a course. In addition, the achievement of specific sales or service goals are acknowledged with Chinese-food or pizza parties; learning—and teaching—is also key to advancing an employee's pay and personal standing in the company.

ICC's learning strategy serves a dual purpose. Jacobi aims to measurably improve his firm's skill base, to be sure; but he also intends to set a tone and constantly challenge complacency—as Jacobi puts it, "comfort."

> The world is changing too fast to stand pat. Growth comes with change, and change is uncomfortable. But if you don't do something every day that you're un-comfortable with, you're losing ground. Five years ago, all our document searches were done manually, on paper. If we told clients they'd have a document in five days, they were delighted. Today, everything is on com-puter. Banks promise three-day loan approval, and we need to respond accordingly. Clients expect overnight delivery—or instant access to our data base.... There's no way you can do today what you did yesterday and sur-vive. If you're comfortable with what you think you know, there's no way you'll be able to meet customers' expectations.[5]

In short, Jacobi sows the seeds for change in his first conversa-tion with job candidates, before they begin their first day on the job. He provides lots of formal and informal training, and he personally harangues, cajoles, and cheerleads his staff. He gives tangible rewards for the learning he demands—by celebrating success, making managers accountable for the development of their staff, and offering front-line employees the opportunity to teach peers and clients.

Sowing can be summed up in a simple gambit used by countless teachers and managers every day: "I'm going to tell you something that may not make much sense right now, but a time will come that it makes sense to you." Brinks Home Security CEO Peter Michel takes a similar tack to prepare employees for change. As he explains:

When I'm mulling over a problem or considering a change in direction, before I know what I'm going to do I'll tell people what I'm thinking. I might say, "You know, I think we need to shift our emphasis from new installations to service. What would that mean to the way you do business?" That does three things—it elicits feedback from employees, it gets people thinking about the business, and it creates a set of expectations that forces me to deliver. If I didn't say anything, I'd never have to do anything. But once I begin to speculate with people, it leads to a shift in strategy.[6]

Of the five skills, it is sowing—and its more dramatic cousin, catalyzing—that triggers thought and action. Sowing is the planting of ideas that learners and mentors will later harvest. Learning leaders, mentors, and managers who ask themselves how to sow wisdom should consider these actions suggested by the stories in Chapter Five:

- Form a clear, consistent message and deliver it at every opportunity.

- Be patient. It's going to take time.

- Eliminate distracting and conflicting messages.

- Begin even before day one. Sowing isn't one act but many.

- Beware. Sowing is an activity that has the potential for manipulation of others and creation of an atmosphere of intolerance.

6

Catalyzing

In chemistry, a catalyst accelerates (or slows) a reaction without being changed itself. In systems theory, catalyzing is a feed forward reaction—the opposite of feedback—where a return of information creates a snowball effect. The idea is to bring a new element into play that makes a system—or people—jump to a higher level of performance. Catalyzing means providing a new and creative approach to a problem by creating the conditions for radical change.

As a skill, catalyzing is different than sowing in timing and directness: leaders and mentors sow when the time is not yet ripe, either because the learner can't yet understand what they're saying or because the time has not yet arrived. Catalyzing, by contrast, is a "hot" tactic; it is used when change is already upon the learner, and there is pressure to quickly understand and apply new knowledge. In catalyzing, there is no previously formulated message; the meaning is in the situation itself.

A philosophy of catalytic change has been late arriving in the history of ideas. The first to use catalyzing as a form of wisdom was Friedrich Nietzsche a mere 100 years ago—and even then, as he said himself, he came too early. It is now respectable to talk of "chaos management." But at the end of the nineteenth century, Nietzsche's attempt to write the "revaluation of all values" and "awaken Europe with a hammer" constituted a radical new way of doing philosophy. It was not until the 1970s that scientists took an interest in disorder as a creative force and developed a mathematics of chaos to describe it.

Many passages in Nietzsche's writings describe the role of the catalyst. For example: "Wisdom: that seems to the rabble to be a kind of flight, artifice and means for getting oneself out of a dangerous game; but the genuine philosopher... lives 'unphilosophically' and 'unwisely,' above all *imprudently*, and bears the burden and duty of a hundred attempts and temptations of life—he risks *himself* constantly, he plays *the* dangerous game..."[1]

Nietzsche exemplifies the catalyst in his way of provoking thought; his pride is to say in a few sentences what others take a book to say—indeed, what others don't say in a book. He takes the part of Dionysus, god of wine and celebration, in loosing the tongue and joyfully letting flow his truths.

Catalytic Enterprise

Catalyzing is the management style that challenges ideas, changes the rules of the game, values chaos, and purposely creates tension and disorientation to accelerate learning. Catalyzing is one of the most difficult skills of wisdom and one of the most antithetical to the traditional concept of orderly management.

The mastery of this process depends to a great extent on using the correct degree of pressure or leverage to change the situation and on choosing the right moment to act. A story told by the Sufis, a mystic order of Islam, illustrates this well. It sometimes happens that a pigeon will fly into a room. In a panic, it will fly and flutter around the ceiling but will be unable to find the window through which it entered. During this time, there is nothing the people in the room can do, although they often try. However, sooner or later the bird will become tired, alight on a beam, and start to calm down. It is at this moment that the wise man acts. With a clap of his hands, he startles the bird, who then flies straight out the window.

For many companies, the necessity of adapting to radically new market pressures has made catalyzing a viable management style. Sun Microsystems is an exemplary catalyst: when Scott McNealy and his friends founded Sun, he was only twenty-seven and recently out of business school. Their strategy was to grab the new workstation niche and quickly take market share by rewriting the rules of the game. So they came up with the radical strategy of licensing their technology to other manufacturers. They believed with more people making Sun-compatible computers more would support Sun software. The open system—a standard feature of today's PC market—was Sun's catalytic invention.

Sun quickly hit a growth rate in the hundreds of percentage points. More impressive still, the company has maintained a catalytic strategy even after reaching the number one position in its market. Catalyzing became a way of life at Sun. For years the company routinely spun off "planets" and "satellites"—independent units given responsibility for a specific project or market opportunity. When asked about the secret of his success, McNealy replies "luck,"[2] and people take this answer as either a joke or a form of modesty. In fact, it comes from a profound respect of the chaotic process that has so far allowed Sun to aggressively compete in a roller-coaster industry.

The Sun example holds three important lessons for catalyzers:

1. Start by upending conventional wisdom or, as Nietzsche said, revaluing values.

2. Sustain the catalytic process by using change to fuel growth.

3. The way to success can't be planned. What McNealy calls luck is largely an ability to act, then adapt to the unpredictable results of the action. .

The Professional Catalyst

Catalyzing is a fascinating phenomenon because it is such a human one. It is the way individuals change systems; it is the very stuff of magic and heroism. In premodern societies, the traditional role of catalyst is that of sorcerers, shamans, healers, and court jesters. In today's marketplace, certain consultants, or gurus, challenge established orders, mock common foibles, and illuminate what their constituents know intuitively. The power of such consultants, defined as change agents, is explained by a growing need for companies to radically and quickly transform themselves.

The best example of a catalyst for change is Tom Peters. In his presentations, he plays the secular evangelist: he sweats, swears, cajoles, begs, and berates his audience to change their ways. He grabs them by the lapels and forces them to see the folly of their ways, using carefully gathered facts and emotionally charged models of innovation and excellence to chart an alternative path for business. His position as an informed and uncompromising outsider allows him to challenge the comfortable assumptions of accomplished leaders.

But why not provoke change from the inside? The reason is that an outsider usually has an advantage in catalyzing a system. The outside catalyst is like the detective in a mystery story. He or she is expendable and unpredictable—free to jolt the system to life and then walk away. The change agent (and this should be remembered in working with consultants!) is not responsible for what the new system will be. Like a lightning rod designed to attract thunderbolts in a storm, thus preserving the building's circuitry, the role of the outside catalyst is to "push the snowball" and then disappear before the situation is stabilized.

You must have two qualities to be an effective outside catalyst. The first is a willingness to challenge assumptions. Of course, challenging does not necessarily mean being right. Indeed, in most confrontations the catalyst must lose—and let the learner find the answer. This often means having enough resistance and courage to confront a hostile group, to say out loud what the problem really is; it means being able to withstand outright rejection and ridicule. Dealing successfully with catalytic situations means being able to have fun under pressure.

Second, catalysts must be able to forget themselves. They must be able to go into a state of passion and act out emotions like anger, sadness, meditation, inspiration. The point, after all, is to lose one's ego. And the lesson to be learned from noncatalysts, those high-powered CEOs sacked during the early 1990s at GM, IBM, American Express, Westinghouse, and Digital Equipment, to name just a few, is that personal ego is a fatal impediment to catalytic change.

These two abilities, to handle confrontation and to submerge one's ego, do not appear on most business school curricula. But they are useful skills in catalyzing companies. For example, in 1985 Jean-Louis Gassée, then CEO of Apple France, wanted to organize a catalytic session for his top twenty managers, whose political infighting was out of hand. As Gassée put it, "They had forgotten that their money is in the customer's pocket."

Gassée designed a meeting during which an evening would be set aside, and the message about the customer was to be understood once and for all. The facilitator he hired for the program was psychiatrist and author R. D. Laing, often called the father of anti-psychiatry, and, as Gassée knew, a most dangerous person to put in the midst of a group. Laing was dynamite; seldom more than two days with him transpired without a fight starting, glass breaking, and blood (usually his own) flowing. But Laing also had the ability to evince extraordinarily rapid change in very disturbed patients and dysfunctional groups. Would his brand of psychiatric shamanism work with executives? Gassée was about the only CEO who would have taken the chance of finding out.

Laing explained what he was planning for the session. Pacing in his hotel room, he said he would use the silent treatment with the group, and proceeded to explain he had learned this directly from its inventor, the psychiatrist Wilfred Bion, at Tavistock. (Bion was a leader of the renowned Tavistock Institute, which developed new therapy techniques and organizational theories in the 1960s.) It was exceedingly simple: the catalyst walks in, sits down, and says nothing. It takes only a few minutes for the reaction to occur. The group could take only three directions. If the executives were in conflict with one another, they would start fighting. Or they would find someone in the group to blame for getting them into this idiotic session. If they were in search of leadership, they would wait and wonder what was going to happen on the supposition that a leader would take over.

So, true to his plan, Laing showed up, had a couple of drinks at the bar while he kept the group waiting, then walked in and sat down. Silence. Then he said: "Why do you think you're here?" and waited some more. It didn't take more than five minutes for the group to catalyze. The executives fought like cats for a while. Then, for the rest of the evening, they talked with great honesty about the problems they were having with one another, why it was not good for the company, and what each was going to change to improve it. Laing himself was even surprised at how quickly the group had moved through the breakdown process to problem solving.

Several days after the meeting, in a corridor at Apple, one of the executives stopped Gassée to ask a question that had been bothering him ever since that evening. "Tell me," he said, "how much did we pay that Scottish son of a bitch to fly in from London and do nothing?"

Catalytic Leader

Within a system, the catalyst has the archetypal role of the hero, the man or woman who assumes a task against overwhelming odds, who defends a strong and fundamental belief. Catalyzing inside an organization—as anyone who has ever filled the role will tell you—is a very risky business. Like the outside catalyst, the catalytic leader must be willing to fight, but in this case his or her credibility depends on succeeding. And where the outside catalyst can be inconsistent and shadowy, the catalytic leader must have the wisdom to keep changing and yet remain constant as the organization evolves. It is a dramatic learning process, with no assurances of continued support for the catalytic leader who takes the helm in chaotic times.

Consider an example from the hotel industry—a business whose failures, takeovers, and hard times have proliferated in recent years. It is fiercely competitive, sophisticated in its use of computers and logistics systems—yet ultimately dependent on the actions of individual employees who deal with the personal needs of customers twenty-four hours a day.

When Reto Wittwer first joined Swissôtel, a five-star, ten-unit Swiss hotel company, he figured, "This is about as close as I can get to job security." The new company was backed by two of the strongest pillars of Swiss industry (Nestlé and Swissair). Swissôtel, with its nationalistic name and logo, represented a statement by the Swiss about their hotel expertise. After all, the Swiss say they invented the hotel industry, and dozens of expensive and exclusive hotel schools offer powerful testimony to their expertise. In the world of hotel management, a Lausanne- or Glion-educated Swiss general manager is considered top drawer at the five-star level. Swissôtel and Mövenpik, however, are the only two Swiss hotel chains.

But Swissôtel just couldn't get its act together. Two presidents were fired in three years; then Wittwer was offered the job. It was a hot seat. Before the ink had dried on his contract, he learned Nestlé had decided to pull out, leaving Swissair holding the bag. Wittwer had to move fast and decisively to prove to his own employees, to Swissair, and, in a sense, to the rest of the hotel world that Swissôtel was a viable operation.[3]

Wittwer decided his first step would be to stake his company on a team of general managers rather than head office executives. He convinced them, during their first time together, to write a mission statement, and they found new faith in Swissôtel through a leader who was "one of them." The second step Wittwer had in mind was to rethink the entire organization supporting the hotels; rather than a stodgy hierarchy, he introduced an organization based on leaders working in networks to reduce costs, accelerate learning, stimulate innovation, and ultimately provide better service to guests.

But meanwhile Swissair, suffering its own industrywide crunch, decided to sell Swissôtel. It soon found a likely Japanese buyer, Aoki Corporation, which had just bought the much larger Westin Group in the United States. For Wittwer, the writing was on the wall: a catalytic president had no place in the Aoki group. He faithfully carried out the legal due process procedures for the buyout and privately started looking around for another job. By now, however, he was feeling bitter that his shot at creating a viable five-star hotel company had been aborted. Wittwer had something to prove.

Then, in the summer of 1990, Saddam Hussein invaded Kuwait; war in the Persian Gulf was imminent—a very risky time for the hotel business. Aoki decided to break off the Swissôtel deal. This left Wittwer with a job, but in a crashed hotel market.

In early 1991, Wittwer proposed a deal to his managers: if Swissair still wants to sell us and you still believe in what we're doing, I'll walk out with you and set up a new company. The managers sent a letter to the Swissair board, which responded by naming a new chairman, a Swissair financier who decided to run the company with little regard for the general managers' aspirations.

Anybody who didn't dance to the new tune would be out of a job. For Wittwer, there was nothing to do except leave, which he did—to begin an even more remarkable turnaround of Europe's largest luxury hotel chain, CIGA, in Italy.

The Swissôtel story illustrates two facts about the catalytic leader that the outside guru doesn't have to worry about.

1. A leader not only has to gain trust, he or she has to sustain it. This ethical challenge means paying attention to detail and giving meaning to actions.
2. An internal catalyst can only succeed by exercising power. Catalytic leadership means risking the leader's reputation on a change he or she can never completely control.

That understanding, a very particular form of wisdom, is what makes it lonely at the top.

Quiet Catalyzer

Catalytic leaders need not rant or rave to ignite a reaction (though that's one way of doing it). But they do need to inspire an emotional commitment from others. It is impossible to be unaffected by the moral power—and working wisdom—of Warden Dennis Luther, for instance.

When a skeptical, even cynical, reporter visited FCI McKean in 1992, he was immediately struck by the quiet confidence of a leader who is both commanding and candid. Luther freely describes the political folly of mandatory drug-sentencing laws that are filling prisons with people who will spend ten, twenty, or thirty years behind bars, giving the United States the dubious honor of locking up a greater percentage of its population than any nation in the world. He is compassionate without being sentimental about the men in his custody. "We're talking about con men and thugs," he points out.

Yet no visitors who spend time talking with McKean's warden, staff, and inmates can leave with their preconceptions intact. Luther demands a new way of viewing the world.

Catalytic Moment

Often, of course, the catalytic moment is thrust on an organization, and managers can only react. Such moments punctuate the life of every organization; how managers become catalysts when the situation demands it makes the difference between renewal and failure.

Diana Edwards played a catalytic role in one of her engagements with a hotel in crisis. The property faced mounting losses—$1 million a year. After years of focusing on the quality of the guest experience and building a culture of uncompromising service, hotel management was under fire from its owners: Why did the hotel spend so lavishly on guest services? Why didn't the food and beverage department generate more revenue? Why were staffing levels out of line with hotels of similar size?

Edwards and management met with the hotel's 300 employees and explained they'd been asked to cut payroll and eliminate many of the amenities guests and staff had come to cherish. Says Edwards, "It was a groundbreaking experience. Nobody had ever sat down with line staff and said, 'You know, we're in trouble. What are we going to do?'"

Employees suggested a number of alternatives: moving the main bar from a dark corner of the lobby to a more prominent location; combining certain jobs and reducing staff levels through attrition; forgoing the free breakfasts served to all employees. Management used the crisis to accelerate a sweeping restructuring of hotel operations. Traditional departments, such as housekeeping, food and beverage, accounting, and reservations, were recombined into four teams based on key processes and customer experiences: prearrival, arrival/departure, stayover, and food/fun. Staff were extensively cross-trained, furthering their understanding of hotel operations, but also allowing them to broaden their skills. Two years later, the hotel earned its first-ever profits.

A self-described renegade, Edwards says she tries to break the mold in her approach. "If nothing else," says Edwards, "crises serve to shake people up. I love it when I'm conducting an orientation and someone says, 'That's all great, but what does it have to do with my job?' I use that as an opportunity to talk about ways to serve the guest—and how that affects everyone's job. Nobody tells anyone anything around here—we talk about it. Everybody learns from that."

Catalyzing is bringing about awareness by fundamentally challenging the status quo. It is a hot tactic that uses change as a learning experience. Learning leaders, mentors, and managers who ask themselves how to catalyze should consider these actions suggested by Chapter Six:

- Challenge assumptions and values to provoke a reaction within the system.

- Trust in chaos: meaningful outcomes emerge by shaking up the organization. This is not a license to mindlessly destroy; wisdom is knowing when and how hard to push.

- Use outsiders as lightning rods in the storm of change, but remember their role is not to clean up the mess they create.

- If you are catalyzing within an organization, maintain credibility by putting yourself on the line.

- Do what works for you; you don't have to rant and rave.

7

Showing

A t first blush, showing seems such an obvious and simple way of transferring knowledge that the reader may wonder why we're devoting a chapter to it. Most of us, after all, are well schooled in showing, from our first day at school. Classroom teaching depends heavily on showing by demonstration. Is not the teacher's job to package information so the learner can follow and reach understanding? Perhaps. But it's easy to confuse the technique of demonstration with the dynamics of learning.

The Method

The source of demonstrative logic can be pinpointed: it was first exposed by René Descartes in 1637, when the philosopher of the *Cogito* explained how he condensed all correct reasoning into a method composed of four simple steps:

1. *Clarity by doubt:* never... accept anything as true... unless it presented itself so clearly and distinctly to my mind that there was no reason to doubt it.

2. *Analysis:* divide each of the difficulties I encountered into as many parts as possible, and as might be required for an easier solution.

3. *Synthesis:* think in an orderly fashion, beginning with the things that were simplest and easiest to understand and gradually... reach toward more complex knowledge.

4. *Quantification:* make enumerations so complete, and reviews so general, that I would be certain nothing was omitted.[1]

Descartes's method became a foundation for scientific thinking; its teachings also took root in the Western mind as institutional reasoning—two notable examples are the invention of bureaucratic procedures by the French and the method of scientific management processes by F.W.B. Taylor in the 1920s. Examine the problem, break it down, analyze each part to find a solution, build the solutions into a new system, and conclude the process with a general review. Such is the method. It can still be found in the planning of any company's yearly budgeting process, and it provides the building blocks of how engineers do problem solving. The method underpins processes like reengineering. In a modified form, the method also dictates how teachers implement learning in classrooms. Learning specialist Malcolm Knowles writes that the basic classroom learning model requires the teacher to answer only four questions:[2]

1. What content needs to be covered?

2. How can this content be organized into manageable units, such as fifty-minute, three-hour, or one-week units?

3. What would be the most logical sequence in which to present these units?

4. What would be the most efficient means of transmitting this content?

Knowles points out that the pedagogical model of teaching neglects the logic of learning itself,[3] which would include steps like setting the proper climate for learning, involving learners in planning what they will learn, engaging them in diagnosing their own learning needs, helping them formulate objectives and design the process, then supporting their learning activity and final evaluation.

So strong is the hold of this logic that many rational people have come to regard any other logic as strange, primitive, superstitious, irrational. Gita Mehta, in her satire of Westerners, sums up what she believes is a Western obsession with rationality: "Heathens do dabble in the irrational, and none more elaborately than Indian heathens who have, in their long evolution, spent a couple of thousand years cultivating the transcendence of reason, another couple of thousand years on the denial of reason, and even more millennia on accepting reason but rejecting its authenticity."[4]

The dilemma of the rational mind is that it does not quite believe the method is the whole story—but can't accept the validity of a different level of perceiving and thinking. The logic of showing is like a glass ceiling that allows you to look into the sky but stops you from climbing outside.

We can distinguish three levels of showing: showing through leadership, the most effective way of transferring knowledge through imitation; rational demonstration, the most useful in the transfer of know-how in training and apprenticeship; and showing as rhetoric, debate among equals.

Imitative Learning

Learning through leadership, setting an example, and showing the way belong to a dimension psychologists call *imitative learning*. This is present in all social interaction. Imitative learning attaches itself to any action—because we naturally do as others do. When we are with others, we read their body language and constantly, unconsciously, interpret meaning.

Research shows, for example, that a baby learns very early how to fix attention and identify the people around it through their physical appearance, gestures, sounds, and facial expressions.[5] This sophisticated, but totally preconscious, learning is practically the only social learning that happens in the first year-and-a-half of childhood. It is at this stage that the mind constructs an idea of an external world, communicates with others, learns the basic logic of life, and acquires language.

We also know from animal experiments that there are a number of mechanisms present in imitative learning. For example, if a rat is placed in a maze behind another rat who knows the way, it will follow the leader. And if the two rats are then put in a maze totally new to both, the relationship of follower and leader is transferred to the new situation. Also, if a rat is alone and must press a lever to drop a pellet of food, it will press the lever much less than if it is placed in front of another rat doing the same thing. The effect of competition makes both rats perform more often than when they are isolated.[6]

These examples make it clear that imitative learning is totally different from demonstrative learning. Imitative learning operates in social interaction, in sports, and in street smarts. It is the learning schools don't teach, even though it is always occurring.

Demonstrative Learning

In the early 1980s, Kathryn Alexander was running a small janitorial business in Oakland, California, when she discovered her main problem was being unable to find good cleaners. The people who wanted to work for her didn't seem to understand the meaning of work. They didn't know *why* they were working. They thought it was for somebody else. They didn't see the benefit of work. For them, work was just a paycheck. Alexander talked to other small business owners and found this was their number one problem, too.

As she had always been interested in education, Alexander decided to tackle this problem at its root—in the schools where young people learn their attitudes about working. Her focus was on the kids that were most likely to drop out of school. Alexander wanted to try something different from the learning associated with blackboards and books and teenagers sitting in rows of desks—a type of learning that was clearly not getting through to these kids. She came up with the idea that the best way teenagers could learn about work was to start their own businesses! Though they might drop out of school, they would have an edge in finding work if they had the right perspective.

In Alexander's "class," students decided what business they were interested in starting, then they went out and found an entrepreneur they could learn from.

Alexander did something clever with high school students who were not doing well in the demonstration mode of education—she let them learn by using imitation as the driving force. These teenagers learned a lot from their mentors and from one another. Moreover, they imitated a projection of themselves as entrepreneurs (first you *are* an entrepreneur and then you begin acting like one).

Alexander has many success stories to tell about her young entrepreneurs, and thanks to her course, many stayed in school. She explains her success very simply: "The difference between what I do with kids and what kids usually get in school is that what I do makes sense to them—they can see its immediate use."

Introducing imitative learning within the structure of a high school program was innovative within the U.S. educational system. Elsewhere, in Germany and Switzerland, for example, the mixture of the two is at the heart of the apprenticeship system, which most students of high school age follow. The apprenticeship system alternates classroom teaching and on-the-job learning with a qualified manager called Meister. The dropout phenomenon is lower in countries that have adopted this double strategy of demonstrative and imitative learning.

Alexander's example offers the following lessons about learning:

- People need to identify themselves with what they are learning. Alexander changed the attitude and self-image of students who had trouble with demonstrative learning by turning them into entrepreneurs.

- Showing should not be limited to formal presentations to passive learners. Alexander's students went out and got people to show them how to start a business.

- Alternating between different logics of learning keeps people interested. The apprenticeship systems of Germany and Switzerland allow students to use a wide range of learning abilities.

The Rhetoric of Showing

Beyond imitation and demonstration is rhetoric, at the heart of the personal interaction of peers in organizations. Rhetoric's rules and techniques were elaborated by the Greek and Roman orators who invented democracy. But rhetoric applies to all interaction, the politics of the family, government, and the company. In common usage, the term *rhetoric*, often preceded by the adjective *hollow*, has come to mean that a speaker does not really believe what he or she is espousing. The challenge facing today's open and participative managers is to both walk the talk—that is, do what they say they will do—and at the same time allow people to talk the walk—that is, question the actions of the company.

One organization that has embraced dialogue and participation—and opened itself to extraordinary internal and external scrutiny—is Levi Strauss. Employees are expected to promote teamwork and trust, recognize and reward others, communicate effectively, embrace diversity, behave ethically, and empower themselves and others. Twice a year, during the performance evaluation process, employees' colleagues and clients provide feedback on how their co-workers embody these corporate values. The re-

views influence pay raises and promotions. But they also open av-
enues of communication between managers and associates and give
people a powerful tool for improving performance—their own and
others'.

The Practical Art of Rhetoric: Talking the Walk

The ability to argue one's convictions in public has an importance
that goes far beyond speech making. It is how individuals *show
themselves* to others.

The Western solution to managing people through open
processes—namely, democracy—was first developed in the agora
of Athens and later in the forum of Rome. Pericles, the founder of
democracy in Athens, first formulated its goals: *promote the best
while ensuring justice*. This goal is no different for managers in
today's organizations.

It isn't easy to democratize an organization. The democratic
management model is definitely *not* modern political democracy
with its party system and elections, where decisions always come
down to a vote. In general, management systems today are more
like the Greek oligarchy—a system where the leaders are ap-
pointed (as with company managers) and wield power as long as
they can get the job done. Oligarchy is not antithetical to democracy; in fact, the two can coexist within an organization. For example, in 1993 Volkswagen decided to appeal directly to workers
through a companywide vote to adopt a four-day workweek rather
than begin massive layoffs in its German factories.

An important step toward the democratization of enterprise
came in the 1980s with the spread of participative management:
the idea that the best means of making sure decisions would be
understood and carried out is to let those responsible for their exe-
cution participate in the decision making.

On another horizon, the debate about giving stakeholders (customers, workers, the local community) a say in how the company

is run alongside the power of the board of directors is an attempt to democratize business. The capable management of many nonprofit organizations, and of socially conscious businesses like Levi Strauss and Ben & Jerry's, again shows that participative management, starting at the top, can succeed. After all, partnerships in family-run businesses and professional firms are structured this way. The point is that participation, whatever the ownership structure, requires decision making, and therefore debate, among peers.

Rhetoric, remember, is a Western invention that makes sense in Western culture. This point is very important in international management as it is not evident that people everywhere in the world assume disagreement and debate result in the best decisions. Studies show such an attitude is, in fact, the exception rather than the rule in management cultures.[7] Japanese management, for example, provides an alternative way of creating open exchange through the concept of social harmony, or *wa*. To produce an atmosphere of harmony where everyone contributes, individuals must work through rituals of respect and constantly solicit others' opinions rather than putting forth their individual opinions. In a management system whose goal is harmony, there will not be open debates, managers will not be asked to be rhetors, and there is no point in talking, in such a case, of democratic management as it is known in the West.

The rhetor's role in Greek democracy was to facilitate wise decision making through debate. The skill involved showing conviction in public and persuading others to make the right decisions. The system led, in Roman government, to a flourishing educational culture where the orator constituted the ideal. Cicero, in the first century A.D., founded this educational system in Rome while building on the earlier examples of Greek political educators, the sophists.

In looking at an organization today one should ask not only whether it is centralized or decentralized, formal or informal, flat or vertical but also should inquire about how many opportunities exist for exercising rhetoric. Are there forums? How many? How many levels of hierarchy can actually argue back and forth? What limits are set on debate and what happens to the decisions that are made by consensus? Is the walk talked and the talk walked? These questions indicate whether democracy is working, whether it is a smoke screen, or whether it is not even an issue. The answers determine the place and the dignity accorded to individuals within the system.

Rhetoric as a Management Process

One of the world's largest hotel groups, Accor, founded in 1964 by co-chairmen Paul Dubrule and Gérard Pélisson, is an example of how rhetoric is learned as a management process. The Accor Group is highly decentralized and comprises more than thirty trademarks: Sofitel and Pullman in the five-star category, Novotel, Mercure, and Altéa with four stars, Ibis and Urbis with three stars, down to the one-star Motel 6 in the United States and Formula One in Europe. Accor is also the world leader in institutional lunch tickets and European leader in institutional catering, and it owns several restaurant companies.

Although the fundamental principle of Accor's management is respect for the individual and independence in doing one's job, democracy came to Accor by accident rather than by any plan of its founders to create a corporate *res publica*. Dubrule tells the story: "We opened our first Novotel with sixty rooms in Lille and the second with thirty-two rooms in Colmar. When I calculated the price of the train ticket between the two cities and added the cost of my own salary, it became apparent that I would be eating up the profits of the new hotel just by doing inspections. So I said to the general manager we hired: 'You are the person responsible for this operation and you do it your own way. All you have to do is send in a report from time to time.'"[8]

So Accor started with a much different management process from the dominant U.S. hotel management system of the time, which depended on heavy procedures and centralized control.

Accor's system allowed its hotels to perform with extremely low profit margins, something the U.S. chains had been unable to realize in Europe.

Accor's system of rhetoric has been based on three principles, the first of which is *delegation*.

Early on, the founders discovered that managers trained in the European hotel schools knew next to nothing about marketing and finance, but they were enthusiastic about learning. Soon, an Accor training bus traveled to each hotel, packed with a trainer, a video camera, and piles of slides on management. So *learning* became the second principle.

The hotel managers, however, lacked the commitment and know-how to provide even the most basic training to their own staffs. This led to the third principle, the Dubrule and Pélisson brand of rhetoric. They built a training center for participative management that allowed learners to work in teams and have fun together. The center became very much a part of the Accor style and attracted bright young people who wanted to learn by *open discussion*.

These three elements of Accor's management made people wiser—and ensured better performance. Soon, Accor began buying out its competitors. As the company grew, Dubrule and Pélisson wanted to underline their commitment to learning by spending $6 million to build a new training center called the Accor Academy. This would be the heart of Accor's culture and would provide state of the art management training. But when the center was finished, the founders discovered it was destroying the intelligence of their management culture. Says Dubrule: "In creating the Accor Academy, we almost ruined what we had built up in the hotels. Suddenly, the managers felt they no longer had to worry about learning, they could delegate it to the professionals and concentrate on short-term business. They became the passive consumers of programs that we would offer them."

Dubrule and Pélisson quickly brought the managers back in as the key decision makers at the academy. The responsibility for designing learning programs—with professional trainers as consultants—belonged to the managers. The professionals at the academy played the role of rhetors since they understood group processes and had a window seat to see where Accor as a company was heading. The capstone of the academy was the presence of the two co-chairmen who would drop in regularly during the lunch break and in the seminars to exchange ideas and find out what was going on in the different companies. The academy became an agora where decisions could be debated and viewpoints argued. As the cultural hub of this large group of companies, it is where Accor defines much of its strategy.

Accor is now growing into an ever larger and more international group in Europe, North America, and Asia. Becoming an international forum of debate in which different cultures will have a more important place is clearly the next challenge for Accor's management.

Showing is a seemingly simple activity, but actually it is extraordinarily complex: At one level it is a question of demonstrative logic, which can be seen in the scientific method, business planning, and standard training procedures. At another level, showing is a matter of imitative learning present in team leadership. At the third level, it is a question of dialogue and open debate.

Learning leaders, mentors, and managers asking themselves how to show wisdom should consider the following actions suggested by Chapter Seven:

- Use as many ways of showing as possible in designing a learning experience. If one level of showing is not working, don't hesitate to switch to another.

- Do not underestimate the power of imitative learning. It is present in everything we do, starting at birth. And do not overestimate the power of demonstrative learning. Not everybody learns what is shown this way.

- Create as many forums for debate as possible—this is the way to participative management.

- Spread responsibility for teaching through dialogue throughout the organization. Train and support managers in that role.

- Use the organization's values and vision as the basis for open debate—and even as an element of employee performance evaluations.

8

Harvesting

H arvesting a vision of the future, helping define a new idea, and
coaxing a product into existence are very much a part of applied managerial technique in learning organizations. Harvesting is
the natural conclusion of the maturation process; the harvester
must successfully guide that crucial moment of bringing something
new into the world.

As a skill of wisdom, harvesting is the opposite of sowing. While
the sower imparts an idea to the learner who is not even aware of
the need for it, the harvester recognizes an idea that is maturing
within the learner's heart or mind. The trick is to bring whatever
"it" is to life without denaturing it. Of the five skills of working
wisdom, harvesting relies most heavily on listening with an
open mind.

Let us first look at the experience of harvesting from the point
of view of the learner. Each of us can probably remember when we
thought we had a great idea and got really excited about it, only to
discover it wouldn't work out. Did we have the proper counselor—
someone to listen, ask the right questions, and guide us? Could we
have avoided wasting time or getting off track? Or were we pushed
into something that really wasn't for us by someone who should
have been more objective and circumspect? There are many cases
of failed harvest. Not all are avoidable, of course, for trial and error
can never be eliminated. But the will to carry on is often dependent

on the attention and respect with which other people treat our ideas.

To harvest individual learning, therefore, we must be totally focused on the other person's attempt to communicate without interjecting our own opinions or cutting off the process through impatience.

The Dream

An important stage in the maturation process of young adults is the definition of one's identity; here, the task of harvesting is, as the painter Gauguin said, to become what you are. Sociologist Daniel Levinson called this life passage "the Dream," a projection of an ideal self in the future that one builds through life experience. In his groundbreaking study of how men mature, Levinson warned that one of the most important choices a young adult can make is to follow that dream or to let it be forgotten and wither away: "Whatever the nature of his Dream, a young man has the developmental task of giving it greater definition and finding ways to live it out. It makes a great difference in his growth whether his initial life structure is consonant with and infused by the Dream, or opposed to it. If the Dream remains unconnected to his life it may simply die, and with it his sense of aliveness and purpose."[1]

Harvesting, although highly personal and even noble as we have seen, is practiced in business at a concrete level. Ideas are vital to any company, and the manager who knows how to bring them into existence can be very successful. Companies also can cultivate ideas as a management process; indeed, the large Japanese companies receive millions of ideas from their employees each year that allow them to make constant incremental improvements in their products, quality, and service. Both quality improvement and innovation depend on harvesting, as the following examples show.

In Silicon Valley, marketing consultant Regis McKenna has developed an impressive clientele thanks to his talent for positioning high technology companies. He built his reputation on work done for two of the computer industry's premier successes, Intel and Apple. McKenna states that when it comes to marketing a new product he draws the elements of positioning from the founders themselves by asking them questions and turning their intuitions into a vision.[2] The marketing strategy for the product flows out of that vision. Every time McKenna begins a new project, his first session is taken up only with listening and taking notes. He insists on the necessity of waiting for spontaneous ideas to emerge. Only at a second stage will he seek relationships and structure in what was said.

Another famous Silicon Valley figure is Arthur Rock, the venture capital magnate who has made a fortune by launching new companies. Rock, who has looked at thousands of business plans for start-ups during his career, estimates the questioning process is the only way to really assess the worth of a new company. Rock states that when he chooses to go with a new business, it is because he believes in the founder of the company, who is much more important than the business plan.[3] He asks questions that have little to do with the business: "Who do you admire?" or "What mistakes have you made in the past and what lessons have you drawn from them?" What Rock is looking for is what he calls the "tactics" of the start-up—how the entrepreneur will behave and what his or her true motivation is. Rock says he will risk his money on the entrepreneur with a burning desire to realize his or her idea, not on someone who thinks he or she is going to get rich from it.

These examples suggest the following lessons about harvesting wisdom:

- You must be open to what the other person is saying without interjecting your own opinions or becoming impatient.

- The harvest starts with a dream or vision. Finding it may take indirect questioning.

- To turn a vision into reality, you must understand the "dreamer's" motivation, life goal, or "burning desire."

Socrates the Master

Harvesting as a skill of wisdom is best represented in the technique made famous by Socrates, which he called *maieutiké* for the Greek goddess of childbirth, Maia. It is little known that Socrates had two ways of questioning: dialectics and maieutics. The first was for his adversaries, a form of verbal judo in which Socrates would draw his opponents into overcommitting themselves and then trip them up. Socrates used this famous rhetorical device of dialectic to devastating effect against those known as sophists, who claimed to teach wisdom to others. The second he reserved for the young men he taught, and his questioning had as its goal the "care of the soul." In a famous dialogue with the young Theatetus concerning the nature of knowledge, Socrates explicitly identifies his art with that of the midwife:[4]

SOCRATES: These are the pangs of labor, my dear Theatetus; you have something within you which you are bringing to the birth.

THEATETUS: I do not know, Socrates; I only say what I feel.

SOCRATES: And have you ever heard, simpleton, that I am the son of a midwife, brave and burly, whose name was Phaenarete?

THEATETUS: Yes, I have.

SOCRATES: And that I myself practice midwifery?

THEATETUS: No, never.

SOCRATES: Let me tell you that I do though, my friend: but you must not reveal the secret, as the world in general have not found me out; and therefore they only say of me, that I am the strangest of mortals and drive men to their wits' end.

Given the educational methods of his time, Socrates' maieutics is an invention of true genius that became a pillar of learning in

Western civilization. Questioning in a relationship of caring for the very soul of another person no doubt constitutes the noblest form of education the West has invented.

Of course, listening techniques are necessary, but the true skill of midwifery lies in this "care of the soul," one's commitment to the relationship and the wisdom to carry out that commitment. Socrates devoted his life to it; he spent his time in Athens observing young learners and asking himself what they carried within them; when he found one who seemed to have an idea, he would begin asking questions. The youth in his entourage feared this power of Socrates as much as they were attracted to it, for he would awaken those "pangs of labor" in them. His power over youth is what eventually led to his being condemned to death by the politicians of the time.

At the end of the dialogue with Theatetus, the young man comes to the conclusion he does not know what knowledge is. His idea is stillborn, but Socrates reminds his young charge the experience will nevertheless make him a better man as, henceforth, he will be soberer, humbler, and gentler to others. As for the art itself, Socrates reveals that the secret is to begin with the conviction that you possess no wisdom; like the midwives of Athens, you must be barren.

> I am not myself at all wise, nor have I anything to show which is the invention or birth of my own soul, but those who converse with me profit. Some of them appear dull enough at first, but afterwards, as our acquaintance ripens, if the god is gracious to them, they all make astonishing progress; and this in the opinion of others as well as in their own. It is quite clear that they have never learned anything from me; the many fine discoveries to which they cling are of their own making. But to me and the god they owe their delivery.[5]

Bunsha

The most interesting example we have found of a management system built on harvesting is that of Bunsha Group, a collection of small companies founded by Kuniyasu Sakai in Japan. Sakai baptized his company after its management system, *bun* meaning to divide and *sha* meaning company.

Figure 8.1 illustrates how *bunsha* works. Each company is divided into departments, and each department functions like a company within the company. For example, the accounting department has the sales department as a client, but it may also sell its accounting services outside the company, in which case the sales department may help them market their services. On the other hand, the sales department may find it more convenient to go outside or do its own accounting. The company, with its internal competition and constant adjustment to opportunities, tends to grow quickly. But just before it reaches its maximum performance potential, in steps Sakai and the company "does bunsha." The manager of the highest performing department is invited to spin off his department into a new company within Bunsha Group, taking with him the employees of his choice. The other companies in Bunsha Group then invest in the new start-up, and the CEO of the parent company becomes chairman of the board of the new company.

Why divide the company? Each manager within Bunsha Group works with what Sakai calls "blue sky" over his head, something rare in Japanese management. Sakai believes not having a hierarchical system over the heads of his managers constitutes the fundamental motivation of the bunsha system and the secret of Bunsha's dynamism. "The managers of large Japanese companies believe the organization is more important than the people that make it up," Sakai explains. "But in my system we count on people. Within even the smallest departments we bring out the 'young lions' and give them every means of succeeding. We don't do it, as in the large companies, with a savant calculation of degrees, career paths, and

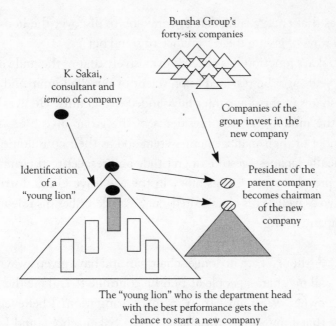

Figure 8.1. *Bunsha* **Harvesting Strategy.**

politics. The way we select them is based on their motivation to take the test of reality and to become their own boss."[6]

At the moment of birth, just before reaching maximum performance, the company can withstand the loss of its best elements being "taken from the womb" by the "young lion" who steals the best employees for the new start-up. The parent company must now reorganize; this galvanizing effect gives the employees who stay in the parent company exciting new opportunities and learning experiences. As for those who have left, they embark on an unparalleled adventure. The system has created forty-six companies, and Sakai believes this is just the beginning.

Today, Sakai spends most of his time searching within the Bunsha Group for those who will create the companies in the future—the young lions. "Though we are highly results-oriented, it is always necessary to cultivate these lions," says Sakai. "Usually you will see it by their superior energy and strong will; but sometimes that energy is hidden. It is my job to discover the lions and find ways of giving them a chance to stand out."

Sakai's function has become exclusively that of the midwife. A few years ago, he resigned as president of Bunsha Group and gave his shares of the companies he founded to a charity. He lives only on the money that the presidents of the group give him as the founder of their management system and as their consultant: in a typically Japanese gesture of gratitude and respect to their master, the presidents pay for his office in the exclusive Ginza district of Tokyo as well as his chauffeured car. Sakai describes his role in the company thus:

> Although I am no longer chairman and have given away all my shares, people at Bunsha continue to call me the owner. Who am I then in this organization? I believe that I am simply the *iemoto* of the Sakai school, and I teach a particular way of managing; I also give advice and, from time to time, produce managers for the company. I often talk on the phone with my presidents, sometimes quite late at night. I'm always available and give my advice freely. Every two months I hold a meeting and talk about my ideas.

Will the system outlive its founder? Is the school really a viable alternative? Here is the somewhat Zen answer of Sakai: "When I'm no longer around, I frankly don't know what is going to happen. All I can say is that my presidents are top-notch and understand the advantages of the system. Whether it will continue after me is, however, an open question."

A Golden Crop

Harvesting the wisdom of people capable of great ideas and bold action who come to you every day—but are seldom asked to do more than what they did the day before—is a manager's ultimate challenge.

As discovered by Dennis Luther, who developed the wisdom of his managers by handing them new assignments, or Bruce Jacobi, who believes people grow only when they are forced to live outside their "comfort zone," or Sakai, who believes people need "blue sky" over their heads, the secret to harvesting is to allow people to develop their own solutions. The payoff is twofold: (1) they reap new ideas and create new businesses, the lifeblood of any enterprise; (2) those who have experienced their own achievements naturally look for ways to help others achieve, which fuels a learning organization.

At Intercounty Clearance Corporation, for instance, knowledge is a business commodity, and the skill of employees is harvested as a source of value to customers. Jeff Boyle was groomed to become leader of a five-person team at ICC, where teaching is a prime indicator of achievement: "If you develop your abilities, you'll be given more opportunities and responsibilities here," he says. "Teaching others is one of the ways you create a career path within the company."[7]

ICC has harvested this activity to create a new value proposition for its clients. The biggest payoff for ICC came when Boyle was asked to teach outside clients. He developed a session specifically for a law firm and delivered a polished, ninety-minute program to fourteen paralegal workers and the firm's managing partner. The presentation established ICC's expertise in an arcane area and has led to a 100 percent increase in business from that client. Says Boyle, "To go to the client, and present with confidence and authority what I know, is the fulfillment, on a personal and professional level, of my four years of experience here."

On a much larger scale, insurance giant CIGNA also looks to its managers to develop employees. Former CIGNA sales manager Heather Gioia (now president of The Tom Peters Group/Learning Systems) describes a learning relationship with a promising sales agent as a breakthrough in her own career. Like most of CIGNA's top sales managers, Gioia spent several days a year conducting formal training for junior sales staff. But her most important teaching—and learning—occurred outside the classroom.

Several years ago, Gioia hired Howard Gruverman, a brash, self-confident twenty-one-year-old who cold-called her to buy advertising design services. She was immediately struck by his natural, if still raw, talent, and hired him to sell CIGNA's HMO plan to large employers. His passion for the work was astonishing, but it also got him into trouble. "He said all the right things," recalls Gioia, "but he lacked discipline. He would say anything to make a customer happy, and then scramble to find a way to deliver. I often wanted to strangle him, but I could never fire him."[8]

Gruverman was on thin ice not only with Gioia but also the secretaries, underwriters, and information managers who had to clean up his messes. The question was not how far he would go in the company but how long he would last. Gioia spent many hours taking him on sales calls, discussing strategy, and explaining the firm's product line, pricing structure, and operations—all of which he mastered. "People come to work with energy and commitment," says Gioia, "and the manager's job is to bring that out, to give them tools, knowledge, and latitude to do the job."

Today, in a company that publicly ranks every salesperson and product line each quarter, he is a top performer for his line and consistently places in the top 10 to 20 percent of salespeople nationwide. But Gioia says she learned as much from Gruverman as he learned from her. "Howard taught me that you have to have passion for what you do, that selling is about having fun, about falling in love with clients. He also showed me that bringing out the best in people is, like selling, based on relationships. It's about trust and friendship."

Harvesting is recognizing someone's idea or vision for something new and helping that person articulate it and apply it in a useful way. Learning leaders, mentors, and managers who ask themselves how to harvest can consider these actions:

- Listen to people and draw out their ideas. This may happen on a mass scale as in a quality improvement system, on a more personal level, or both.

- Train managers in the art of questioning and dialogue (the Socratic method) so good ideas don't get squelched.

- Allow those who have ideas to participate in making them into real products, services, or business.

- Get people who have benefited from your harvesting strategy to go out and help others.

- Take a risk on people with potential.

Part III

. . . .

Strategic Imperatives for

Implementing Wisdom

9

The Leadership Imperative

Designing successful learning strategies means leaders must know enough about learning to make decisions about their goals for the organization. They must identify their key wisdom needs and resources. They must adjust learning to innovation and changes. They must know what activities to plan and invest in. Finally, leaders must know how to communicate a commitment to developing their people.

The examples of working wisdom given in previous chapters suggest two types of learning management: *personal learning tactics*, the five skills used to transfer learning and promote individual growth; and *organizational learning strategies*, the architecture of the learning organization. The five skills can be carried out in parallel and at differing intensities according to the learning situation. But to successfully apply these skills, leaders must understand learning strategy.

A model of learning strategy is Motorola, considered by many to be the premier learning company in the United States. When its leaders looked at its future human resource needs in the late 1980s, they realized they had to become a much more knowledge-based company.[1] Motorola developed a "critical path" strategy to create a broad-based culture of participation and quality, minimize differences of rank and status, and provide certification for learning. To foster the skills needed to manage with more autonomy within their teams, Motorola University taught critical thinking and problem-solving skills throughout the company's six business units. Leaders also asked managers to describe how key positions on their team were going to change, what competencies and skills would be required within five years, and if those skills existed within the company.

Framing a Learning Strategy

We have framed organizational learning strategy at the level of top management as having six critical tasks and one practical bias, a bias for action best stated by Tom Peters and Bob Waterman.[2] That is, sooner rather than later you must put your grand strategy to the test. The six tasks are:

1. Set strategic targets for learning in relation to your long-term, competitive strategy.

2. Assess the value of strategic knowledge and define the life cycle of knowledge turnover.

3. Define your organizational structure to support your learning strategy.

4. Structure learning into employment contracts and promotion procedures.

5. Identify dominant learning paradigms, models, and attitudes within the organizational culture; decide which should be un-learned and what new paradigms to integrate into the culture.

6. Audit the efficiency and quality of training programs and learning networks within the organization and benchmark the data against competitors.

Setting Strategic Targets for Learning

When strategizing learning, the leaders of an organization should ask, What do we need to learn as a company? This question is part of a larger discussion of other challenges facing the company and of a general assessment of the business environment. Framing business strategy in terms of learning means managers must make sure people know and understand what is happening in the organization and in the industry. Preparing people for change is not something that can be done overnight.

When Antoine Guichard wanted to move Casino from a provincial supermarket operator to a major player in a European alliance, he set learning objectives for his company and created a training institute to make it happen. When Dennis Luther wanted to make FCI McKean into a place of learning for staff and inmates, he set objectives for management to master career-building projects and to promote trust. At Brinks Home Security, members of the executive committee, which includes the head of training and human resources, constantly challenge one another to identify business and learning opportunities.

But however it's done, learning targets should end up in all strategic planning. This has an added advantage: it allows those who are implementing learning to help set the strategic goals.

Assessing Strategic Knowledge and Knowledge Turnover

Putting a price tag on learning is difficult unless the value of a particular type of knowledge or expertise to the organization can be identified.

When Spectra-Physics sought to restructure its manufacturing processes and compensation policies around employee skills, it put a relative value on every job in the plant. Mastery of more complex tasks, such as robot operation, as measured by the time necessary to gain proficiency, was essential to job advancement. A highly skilled, flexible workforce was essential to the company's competitive strategy, so it devised ways to measure the value of knowledge; it then provided incentives for workers to direct their own learning, master multiple skills, and keep those skills current.

A simple way to determine value is what Intercounty Clearance Corporation does: when it develops a valuable new competency inside the corporation, it sells it.

As the Bunsha Group example shows in its bunsha process, this external marketing can be reproduced by divisions, business units, and departments.

Defining the Optimum Learning Structure

Organizational structure, the object of much focus in management literature, is rapidly changing. Creating a learning organization isn't a matter of redrawing the organizational chart.

We have already seen learning organizations that create job mobility through cross-functional projects and teams, as Spectra-Physics. Again, Bunsha Group is perhaps the most creative in implementing its "blue sky" philosophy of making any promising manager into an entrepreneur. Or we can think of Chiat/Day's transformation of its head office into a university-like structure or Bouygues's creation of an internal order of master construction workers to coach others.

Each organization is different and must find its own best organization based on its culture, resources, and strategy. In a recent book on learning organizations, Karen Watkins and Victoria Marsick speak of "sculpting" the organization, using the metaphor of chipping away at a mass of stone until it reveals the form that fits the vision of the artist.[3] Organizations should be crafted until the potential for informal learning is realized in formal work processes.

Structuring Learning Contracts

Management should structure learning requirements into job specifications linked with bonuses and promotions. We have seen an excellent example of this with Spectra-Physics. In its Proskill program, employees are required to master a portfolio of manufacturing skills in which they are cross-trained by peers. Their proficiency is certified; and wages, raises, and promotions are tied to learning.

Raychem's Career Center helps employees manage their professional development and pursue opportunities internally. And at Swissôtel's Beijing hotel, local Chinese can negotiate a fair deal that gives them valuable training in return for staying on the job until they have completed the course.

The advantage of a contract is to know exactly what is expected by each party to meet the required skill and competency levels. The advantage for managers is to be able to plan learning more effectively and to put learning performance on the same basis as work performance.

Identifying Learning Paradigms, Models, and Attitudes

Top managers have an increasing responsibility to drive organizational change. It is therefore important to recognize which models, attitudes, and values dominate the organizational culture and to evaluate their harmony with the new strategy. Are they a help or a hindrance? In many cases, new work models require unlearning the previous paradigms that people in the organization had thought normal. We saw how Casino changed its paradigm of a strong centralized headquarters built around a family business and introduced the model of a European partnership of supermarket chains. We've also seen how Kathryn Alexander was able to substitute the paradigm of learning as an entrepreneur for the paradigm of classroom learning for kids with difficulty in school. Perhaps the most dramatic paradigm shift we've studied is what Luther did at FCI McKean to transform an environment of punishment to one of personal progress.

We've seen several large organizations that are unable to change simply because they embrace a motley collection of paradigms in different divisions or in the minds of their top executives. In such companies, it's impossible to define a common strategic direction. That's why paradigms are a leadership concern.

Selling new paradigms within an organization is a question of addressing attitudes and teaching a new way of working. Take the example of the network paradigm used in organizational theory. If people are really expected to understand how superior performance can come out of networks, they must be given time to explore the whys and wherefores of what a network is. This takes time and is one area where classroom teaching can really make a difference. Strategizing new attitudes and behaviors may require a more psychological approach, but people still need a framework for understanding something radically new and time to integrate it into behavior.

Auditing Organizational Learning

Organizational learning is difficult to improve if it can't be assessed. Some of the techniques used to measure quality can also be applied to learning—defining minimum levels of performance, analyzing root causes of failures, and so on. Audits can also be used to get at the elements of learning activity. We know of one organization that monitored the number of parties held in its offices to see if people were communicating informally.

Many organizations try to audit their learning systems, identify strategic learning goals, and communicate to work teams the need for organizational and personal renewal. Motorola's training and unit managers systematically evaluate participant satisfaction, degree of learning, and application of skills to the workplace. Raychem and Spectra-Physics rely primarily on managers and employees to assess individual learning and identify key learning needs. Independent, nonprofit organizations, such as the Center for Learning Metrics in Chicago, Institute for Research on Learning in Palo Alto, California, and Center for Learning Assessment at MIT, are doing research into learning measurement and benchmarking for different learning programs.

Although audits can measure a lot—even the "delight" of learning, much as quality audits have begun measuring "customer delight"—some learning processes simply fall outside the domain of incremental learning audits. This is particularly true of global companies that invest massive resources to turn around their operations and culture. When Jack Welch took over at General Electric, he refused to answer questions about how much he was investing in GE's Crotonville management learning center at Croton-on-Hudson, New York. Jan Timmer of Philips would say only, "It's worth it" to describe his ambitious Centurion project to redirect his organization. These leaders avoided debates about cost to focus attention on the vision of their learning programs. Nonetheless, both Welch and Timmer set up teams to monitor whether change was actually occurring in divisions worldwide.

Implementing a Bias for Action

Developing learning strategies is a laudable pursuit. So are self-directed work teams, TQM, and process reengineering. But they are not ends in themselves. The goal of these efforts—and the basis on which we must judge their success—is the sustainable success of the organization in the marketplace. To justify the time and resources invested in any learning strategy—and to win continuing support for the strategy itself—we must demand meaningful results. Learning leaders bring learning in line with global corporate strategy and prove themselves by hitting performance targets that wouldn't be possible without significant learning.

Douglas Smith, consultant and coauthor of *The Wisdom of Teams,* offers some wisdom of his own for translating learning strategies into tangible action: "The closer people find themselves to a true performance challenge that matters to themselves, the organization and shareholders, the more they are able to work in real time, with access to resources to meet the challenge, the more they will learn."[4]

Smith cites the example of Dun & Bradstreet Information Services N.A.—a $700 million division of the business-information giant and the world's largest credit reporting agency. After the 1990 merger of several business units, Mike Berkin, senior vice president for performance quality and customer service and Smith's client, created a "bottom-up" strategy.

The effort began with a cross-functional committee of department heads undertaking a ten-month "period of enlightenment" during which they visited other companies, read, studied, attended conferences, and shared what they learned with their peers and top management.

Out of the period of enlightenment came the conviction that any change efforts should incorporate four principles:

1. Focus teams on an "urgent and compelling performance-improvement opportunity."

2. Build on early, quick success, rather than first training everybody in the organization.

3. Tailor training to the needs of the team members and their immediate goal.

4. Circumvent the cynics and skeptics by avoiding buttons, slogans, public announcements of strategy, and other trappings of a program launch.

Smith and Berkin also used familiar tactics to achieve their goals—they catalyzed learning in a controlled environment (a business unit), then sowed the process throughout the company. The key, says Smith, was integrating learning directly into the workplace.

To kick off the process, Berkin's team identified a business opportunity worth millions. Though the company had just reduced the time it took to gather and analyze the creditworthiness of an unrated business from ten to seven days, that was still too long for D&B clients who were waiting to ship an order or extend credit to a new customer. A cross-functional, front-line team at a data-gathering center in Greensboro, North Carolina, volunteered to tackle the problem. Their goal was to cut the process to just three days within eight weeks.

The team examined the entire operation in their office, consulted with functional experts from other parts of the company, and made several quick, incremental changes. Within four weeks, report-processing time had been cut to less than two days. Then, they presented their results to senior management and front-line staff doing similar work in the firm's sixty-some field offices.

The catalyzing tactic induced people at the front line to demand training and participation to meet the challenge. In rolling out the effort in successive waves throughout the organization, D&B used front-line facilitators trained in the "breakthrough strategy."[5] Today, it has more than 100 facilitators companywide; each is available to other units seeking help. After three years, Berkin points to more than $52 million a year in gains, most in new revenues generated by project-improvement teams. Says Berkin, "We used the breakthrough strategy to harvest those opportunities."

D&B's strategy succeeded because, as Smith reminds us, leaders clearly tied learning to tangible, sustainable results. But Berkin and his colleagues also addressed the six tasks of an organizational learning strategy:

- Setting strategic targets for learning (the "period of enlightenment")

- Assessing the value of knowledge (the competitive advantage of faster turnaround time)

- Defining a structure to support learning (the cross-functional project teams)

- Structuring learning into work roles and promotion procedures (the 100 in-house facilitators who circulate throughout the organization)

- Identifying dominant learning paradigms (the breakthrough strategy of small, visible wins)

- Auditing the quality of training (the $52 million gains attributable to the program)

The Managerial Imperative

Given the time and performance pressures we all face, we too often believe developing the people who work with us is an extra—something we can do if we have a proclivity for it—provided it doesn't stop us from meeting short-term objectives. Seldom do we structure work to support the transfer of organizational knowledge and know-how. In a learning organization that considers working wisdom a vital asset, this is simply not good enough. To be effective, we must know how to manage learning management and define the different roles of the learning manager—coach, mentor, facilitator. These roles do not necessarily correspond to the classical definition of manager; in fact, regional salespeople, executive assistants, technical experts, and anybody with wisdom in the organization plays a learning management role. For strategic purposes, it is useful to group these roles under the generic heading "learning manager" in order to allocate resources to the learning function.

Many ways of supporting learning managers can already be found in organizations. Table 10.1 shows how these resources come into play for each of the five tactics of wisdom.

Table 10.1. Managing Learning Managers.

Accompany	The use of consultants to support learning managers is becoming widespread. Managers are themselves supported in career search by headhunters, in job searches by outplacement agencies. Professional organizations for small businesses sometimes provide networking systems where members audit and consult each other.
Sow	In turnaround situations, CEOs sow the seeds of change to the whole company. Often consultants are used to indicate a new paradigm emerging in the company even before the policy has been announced.
Catalyze	Work in change management involves mastering catalytic situations. Consultants used as change agents impart catalytic strategies to managers. Leaders who have successfully turned around an organization become teachers and write books about their methods.
Show	Committees and meetings provide the occasion to debate issues.
Harvest	Companies have been generally poor at harvesting the wisdom of managers in a practical, concrete way. Knowledge-based organizations often value wisdom, but that wisdom is often not managed systematically. The exception is the research organization or professional service firm that positions the accomplished master as an extraordinary asset.

Do We Need Managers?

Some of the world's most eminent business leaders, from Japanese industrialist Konosuke Matsushita to GE chairman Jack Welch, confirm the view that effective managers must manage learning. Even as Welch set about "delayering" and challenging the position of managers at GE, he still respected the "soft" skills of managers: "In the past, many staff functions were driven by control rather than adding value. Staffs with that focus have to be eliminated. They sap emotional energy in the organization. As for middle managers, they can be the stronghold for the organization. But their jobs have to be redefined. They have to see their roles as a combination of teacher, cheerleader, and liberator, not controller."[1]

Learning leaders, coaches, mentors, and learning guides can use the five learning skills to facilitate the day-to-day development of individuals, but they must also be able to implement organizational learning strategy.

At LifeScan, a fast-growing Johnson & Johnson subsidiary, managers regularly review not only employees' performance but also their development goals. They reconcile and align both corporate and personal strategies.

After employee-satisfaction surveys identified a need for ongoing employee development, Nan Watanabe, manager of organizational development and training and development, and Danette Taylor, manager of employee relations, formulated a three-part Individual Development System:

1. *Goal setting and action planning.* The company's strategic focus drives annual departmental and individual goals.

2. *Individual development planning.* Based on self-assessment, manager's feedback, and dialogue about the skills to be cultivated, it involves very personal discussions with the manager of each associate's aspirations, motivations, personal goals,

and values. This is then structured as a personalized development plan for the year.

3. *Performance evaluation.* Each year, in agreed-upon areas,
   employees and their managers are accountable for improving
   their performance.

Says Watanabe: "We have to ask ourselves, as an organization, 'Can
we afford employees who don't want to develop as individuals?'"

Managers are accountable for how well they help others develop, but the impetus and real accountability for that development
come from the employees themselves. What's made clear, says Taylor, is that managers are expected to do "whatever is most expedi-
ent, effective, and efficient to promote learning" through strategic
discussions with employees.[2]

Defining New Roles for Managers

The vast restructuring of organizations in North America, Europe,
and Japan makes clear that managerial work has to be redefined and
that managers will be expected to meet the needs of a learning organization. How? We propose a new context for analyzing this problem, encompassing four key contributors to a learning organization:
business managers, experts, learning managers, and *project consultants.*
Each role may be defined by a specific agreement addressing such
questions as, Do we pay managers for performing a task or are we
asking them to provide knowledge? Is a manager handling a core
responsibility or providing an independent service? Once these dis-
tinctions have been made, we can decide whether we need managers to be committed full time to the organization, have part-time
contracts, or outsource the job completely.

Business Managers

Like the expert, the business manager is a familiar figure to most
organizations—the department head, team leader, general man-

ager, or director responsible for the financial and operational health of his or her unit. But at least three important changes are likely:

1. Managers can expect to see much more of their pay based on performance.
2. More internal business activities will be restructured as independent profit centers—or outsourced entirely.
3. Business managers will have to contract learning resources.

In a hotel, for example, rather than having a food and beverage department, bars and restaurants are broken into small businesses, as are its laundry service, front desk, and conference facilities. In a computer company, each functional department becomes a business with a bottom line—marketing, after-sales service, software development, and so on. Managers' salaries vary according to performance, with bonuses and profit-sharing schemes providing powerful incentives.

In a learning organization, each business manager of a unit is responsible for maintaining and improving expert knowledge, developing people, and solving problems. Top management gives business managers strategic guidelines concerning objectives, investment, management systems, standards, and new projects and practices.

Experts

Every organization has its experts—those who produce specialized knowledge essential to the organization. It may be the senior scientist of an aerospace firm or the administrative assistant who knows the ins and outs of government procurement. The role encompasses key staff positions, specialists, researchers, and professionals—controllers, lawyers, computer experts—and, in general, people whose knowledge or know-how is so important that keeping them in the organization is vital.

For service-based organizations, certain client-contact positions are key to customer service, such as an airline's check-in counter. These people are also experts. In industrial organizations, the experts are usually organized into research and development units.

The decision to structure someone's job as expert rather than consultant, or even as head of a business unit, is an important one. For example, some firms' R&D departments have been converted into profit centers. Some experts are used on a consulting basis. There is no one best solution, and personality is an issue. Some experts just can't work in a team; others can't work without an office and a secretary; still others prefer to teach part-time and manage a portfolio of activities.

Learning Managers

In yesterday's organizations, a certain percentage of any manager's job was supposed to be devoted to people development, but many managers only paid lip service to the philosophy and left the task to the human resources department.

In our view, this imperative requires a specific job: it is in this category that we would place titles like coach, mentor, and learning guide, under the generic title of learning manager. Learning managers develop individuals as clients and do so with the investment that top managers devote to people development.

Learning managers should be paid according to learning contracts targeting specified, if not measurable, results. If the client learners don't feel they are being helped sufficiently, the learning manager loses the client. If the learning programs don't meet targets, the manager loses renewal of the contract.

Shifting traditional managers into this role is possible if learning managers have their own support system. Training activities may be converted into a corporate university where learning managers can have a home and where they can work together. Still, the lion's share of development should take place at work. Only then can the skills of wisdom be leveraged to their full potential.

Top managers should decide whether to keep this function in-house or give it to outside professionals. Business unit managers should decide what works best for their unit.

Consultants

While learning managers are paid to implement learning strategy as a service, consultants provide other business resources. Consulting, as defined here, comes in three forms: solving problems, implementing new processes and procedures, and setting up new businesses. Often consultants and learning managers team up to carry out projects.

Consultants are under contract with pay tied to end results. Contemporary consulting packages, such as temporarily running a new business or being paid according to the profits generated, can be adopted. Consultants also need organizational support. Those operating inside the organization may work in consulting firms similar to external firms.

With this matrix structure, the manager's role in the organization becomes more flexible and accountable. Figure 10.1 is a convenient way for learning strategists to decide how to allocate their managerial resources. The vertical axis shows the relative weight to be given to long-term wisdom as compared to short-term performance. A typical knowledge-based organization, such as a consulting firm or high-tech start-up, would focus on the top half of the grid; a transaction-based organization, such as a supermarket or restaurant chain, would concentrate on the lower half. The horizontal axis allows strategists to "rent or buy" their learning services. On the left side of the grid would be those managers whom an organization would want to keep on salary (although some experts can also be outside the firm); on the right side, resources would be planned and budgeted as an outside service.

Of course, wise managers will play different roles during their careers. In fact, the ideal development path for a top executive is to move around in all four boxes of the management matrix.

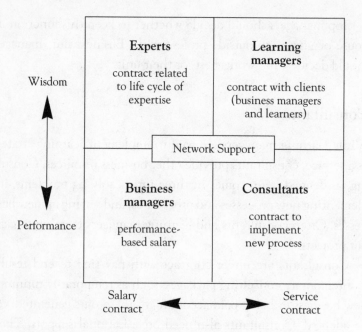

Figure 10.1. Learning Management Matrix.

A dramatic example of how functional managers are being asked to shift into the role of service provider came from IBM's deep restructuring in 1992 when the company reorganized its training department as Skill Dynamics (now called IBM Education and Training), a subsidiary chartered to compete in the open market. Suddenly, IBM's trainers and course developers had to market internally and externally, and many became independent consultants who contracted with IBM.

Henry S. Miller, formerly an in-house trainer based in IBM's San Jose storage products division, now works as a free agent for dozens of high-tech firms and training companies, including IBM, which has at times subcontracted his services back to the very units where he used to be on staff. Says Miller: "It's easy for companies to tell their departments to go out and sell their services to the outside world but the staff soon discovers it's a very different game in terms of entrepreneurial skills, mindset, logistics, and finances."[3]

Now, even when teaching a course he developed and delivered as an IBM employee, Miller finds subtle but important differences. "I was teaching the same material in the same classrooms, with the same support people," he says, "but there were no house politics— no meetings, agendas, or administrivia. I could focus much more closely on the learning. The amount of time I can spend on customer-specific, revenue-generating events is probably 90 percent; as an in-house trainer, I was lucky if it was 5 percent."

11

The Network Imperative

I n any organization, how people develop on the job is so spontaneous and fluid that nobody really knows who is involved or
where the knowledge flows. This informal quality of learning is a
strength, but managing these networks is very different from managing a hierarchy. Learning at the personal level is based on informal relationships and happens as opportunities for learning present
themselves. Attention to flows and informal roles people play in an
organization is necessary in order to manage learning effectively.
In short, top managers now must better understand how networks function and manage them as their principal development
organization.

To complete the learning strategist's question, What does our
organization need to learn for tomorrow? we also need to ask, How
do we learn today? We can analyze the hidden activity of learning
according to the following specific characteristics of networks:

- The learning content that flows through the network:
  What are people learning?
- The roles of people in the network: Who is mentoring
  and who is taking responsibility for development?
- The structure of the development network as a whole:
  hierarchical or flat, closed or open, centered or diffuse,
  and so on.

- The tactics of development within the network: sowing ideas, accompanying, catalyzing, harvesting, and others.

- The resources used for learning: meetings, tools, or investments.

Learning leaders must make sure the organization supports the informal learning that occurs in networks and that it is pertinent to the overall strategy. It is important to note that not all networks are propitious for an organization, nor do they automatically promote learning. Old boy networks, bureaucratic networks, and information-retention networks have to be eliminated for the learning organization to take hold. At this point, we should clarify what constitutes a healthy learning network.

A well-managed learning network is one in which members agree to common strategy, goals, principles, methods, and rules for exchanging knowledge, skill, and resources. What drives the network is a common learning philosophy that answers the question, Why do we want to learn?

Most learning networks in work organizations are still at the trial-and-error stage, a point eloquently made by John Sculley, former chairman of Apple Computer, who compares today's organizational architecture to building cathedrals:

Organization design today is like building a cathedral a thousand years ago. The master builders of the cathedrals would have a wonderful vision of what they wanted a cathedral to look like, but they knew that the technology was not developed enough to actually build the cathedral they envisioned. They also knew they would be dead before it was completed. And yet they started out believing that the technological problems would be resolved in the hundred years or more that it would take to complete the cathedral. When they built vaulted ceilings for cathedrals, most of them fell down because nobody knew the engineering principles involved. But through trial and error, making mistakes, they eventually got it right. The most innovative cathedrals couldn't possibly have been built if they'd been designed from the start.[1]

In other settings, for example in the exchange of scientific research and in the professions, learning networks have a head start. One here-and-now application of learning technology is Lexis Counsel Connect, an on-line network that is changing the way some of the nation's top law firms do business. A joint venture between Time Warner affiliate American Lawyer Media and the information service Mead Data Central, Counsel Connect started as a clubby private service linking several big-name New York law firms. Today, with more than 10,000 users worldwide, it combines a "traditional" data base of legal research material, with more than eighty-five on-line conferences dedicated to different legal specialties, and an e-mail messaging system. The system allows, for instance, an environmental litigator in New Jersey to query colleagues on a narrow point of law and receive detailed answers within twenty-four hours. In addition to personal e-mail from other lawyers throughout the country, the litigator may find waiting in his or her electronic mailbox a personalized bulletin featuring news clips, legal citations, and memos tailored to his or her specific request.

Counsel Connect "will free—indeed, require—lawyers to do what is intellectually rewarding...to be rewarded for what they know, not for how well they can leverage their troops, [and] to be rewarded for value delivered to clients rather than time spent on problems," according to American Lawyer Media CEO Steven Brill.[2] Open only to attorneys, the network allows participants to adapt relevant work done by colleagues in other firms. It meets two criteria, reports Brill, that clients use to measure the value of professional services: "(1) speed of response and (2) the smartest possible adaptation of work already done to help solve new situations and new problems." Counsel Connect is effectively a self-managed network: the users write the rules and determine the value of the information traded. Subscribers pay royalties to those who contribute material to the network, creating a market for legal talent. Counsel Connect also serves as a virtual classroom for continuing legal education seminars, which lawyers otherwise would need to travel to attend. It establishes learning networks as a new collaborative vehicle for knowledge workers—a vehicle that opens new channels for scholarly and professional writing and offers immediate, unfiltered feedback from peers.

When dealing with knowledge networks, it's not who you are but what you know that confers status.

Human Networking

Networking is another way of putting people together. In the 1970s when Tetsuzo Kawamoto was given the mission of creating Japan's first City of Science in Tsukuba outside Tokyo, he asked himself how he could design a learning community. Kawamoto had been a professor of geography, which helped him organize the actual layout of Tsukuba. He knew, for example, that teaching is not the only way young researchers learn from practicing scientists; coaching and informal discussion are also key learning activities in research projects. From personal experience, Kawamoto figured that science professors wouldn't want to hang around classrooms after they had finished teaching. So he built inexpensive restaurants and cozy inns close to the housing area to allow professors and students to gather for a meal or a drink and continue talking informally.

In addition, Kawamoto knew it would be important to promote cross-learning among researchers in the different scientific disciplines. So he set up a data base for students. When they arrived at

Tsukuba, students entered their answers to three simple questions into the data base:

1. What is your field of research?
2. What tools and techniques do you use?
3. What are your hobbies, sports, and pastimes?

Kawamoto knew useful exchange could begin within these parameters and could lead to surprising encounters. For example, a physicist and a biologist might like tennis and also use lasers in their research: if they got together for a game, they would start talking about lasers and—who knows?—maybe make some interesting connections in their research.

The key to Tsukuba is that Kawamoto was an organizational strategist rather than a manager. He designed learning encounters but did not control the details.

Auditing Learning in Networks

The Institute for Research on Learning, in partnership with companies like Xerox and Sun Microsystems, has closely observed the details of personal networking in the workplace. In the organizations IRL has studied, learning is an ongoing, inevitable, and fundamentally social activity that occurs in "communities of practice"—informal, overlapping groups based on professional and personal affinities. These communities cut across formal organizational structures and are bound together through the shared experiences and values of their members. There is always, for example, an "in" group of programmers at a software house or salespeople in a consulting company.

As people earn acceptance in a community, they figure out what they need to know to do the job—not just in terms of technical requirements and policies but, more importantly, who knows what and how many dumb questions they can ask. The vitality of each

organization's communities of practice and the fluidity with which
people and ideas can move between them largely determine the
depth of organizational learning that will occur in the workplace.

Within these communities, three conditions must be met by
members, and, according to IRL research, the management of learning often comes down to the management of these conditions:[3]

- *Legitimacy.* Members must have personal and professional credibility and standing with the group, usually
  earned by their presence and participation.

- *Peripherality.* Members must be able to live and learn, at
  times, on the edges of the group's activity. People need
  opportunities to observe, assimilate, and test new ideas
  outside the limelight.

- *Participation.* If meaningful learning is to take place,
  learners must be active participants in actual work.

One reason formal training courses sometimes fail to achieve results, say IRL researchers, is that they are not tied to the real work
of people in the organization.

The social and participative nature of learning at work has
important implications for team leaders. If they determine the conditions for learning are present, the most effective thing they can
do is let the natural learning of the group unfold spontaneously
through people's engagement in the work itself. If, on the other
hand, leaders and managers see a problem in any of the three enabling conditions, they must marshal learning resources and inter-
vene tactically to get the group going.

Leaders can, for example, accompany a new member of the
group by saying, "We don't expect you will be able to perform 100
percent from day one. It may take time to figure out how things
work here; please ask if you have questions." Thus, they help foster
the peripherality necessary to learning. Susan Stucky, IRL's associ-

ate director, suggests several methods for managers to support the communities of practice that form networks of learning in organizations:

- Think about the patterns of participation and inter- action among your team and how you can encourage participation.

- Create opportunities and occasions for people to get to- gether over real work.

- Allow people the shared time and/or shared space essential to collaboration.

- Cross-fertilize thinking by, for instance, having junior- level staffers observe the work of senior executives.

- Look for those rare people who have legitimacy in a number of communities and can move freely between them, brokering ideas; they are ideal learning leaders— and they usually don't fit the profile of the model manager.

Finally, Stucky offers an important warning to those who would treat networking as a straightforward "knowledge transfer," using information technology or training. "Learning—or practical wisdom—is the ongoing practice of what you do; it's not something you can package neatly and transfer to another person."

Information systems, for example, are fine for broadcasting tech- nical content, direct inquiries, or commentary, but they are inca- pable of conveying the true craft honed through years of experience on any job. Stucky reminds us that a sense of ambiguity, intuition, poetry—in other words, the language of wisdom—is conveyed only by the personal engagement and collaboration of people work- ing together.

12

The Technology Imperative

Distance learning, multimedia, hypertext, groupware, interactive videodisks, electronic highways, and virtual reality make learning technology a necessary consideration in any organization. Learning technology is what is driving the knowledge turnover rate because information can be distributed as fast as it is produced. It also has an enormous impact on learning costs. Traditional learning is a people-intensive, low-tech activity, as a glance at the budget of any university or training institute will confirm. But technology is already having an impact on the dynamics of learning.

Posteducation Learning Technology

Not only does learning technology have an impact on how knowledge is distributed and promise lower costs compared to teaching, but also these new technologies are generating new thinking into learning itself. The logic of demonstration used in teaching is being replaced by multiple logics. As early as 1991, Texas authorized the replacement of certain textbooks by interactive videodisks in its high schools. At the Massachusetts Institute of Technology, research into multimedia learning has been going on since the early 1980s when companies such as IBM and Digital Equipment granted MIT $50 million to launch its Athena project.

A later spinoff of Athena, the Center for Educational Computing Initiatives, deals specifically with innovations in learning. Research Associate Ben Davis believes learning technologies will have as much impact on our perceptions of the world as the microscope and telescope did in early science. MIT now encourages professors to write course material using AthenaMuse software; these multimedia packages provide alternative learning paths, and the focus on learning rather than teaching changes the traditional relationship between professor and student. Davis, a former art professor, finds it reminiscent of teaching creative arts.

> When I was an art professor, I was confronted with the problem of how to grade students who were doing creative work. I came to understand that it should be based on a self-assessment of learning and that my own judgment as a teacher should be focused on what I call quality of interest. I never had a problem with grading based on self-assessment except in cases where a student was doing poor work and knew it. If I thought his quality of interest was poor and it was like pulling teeth to get the student to admit it, I'd give a poor grade—not so much on the work itself as for his low motivation in learning. To teach art consists essentially of confronting students with how they are learning to be creative. Likewise, the best professors using multimedia are essentially preoccupied with ways to make learning more interesting...and they continuously learn from how their students are learning. Our art is touching the sensitivity of learners by creating moments of inspiration using learning technology.[1]

Learning can be an adventure, a quest to understand in which one navigates through information. It can be a way of linking yourself to just about anybody with whom you need to dialogue. It can be a packaged learning experience on a CD-ROM with moving images, sound, and interactivity. The possibilities are mind-boggling, and the question immediately arises, Will we even need real people to animate our learning programs? What is the role of wisdom in technology?

Jean-Louis Gassée, formerly vice president responsible for marketing, production, and research at Apple Computer, is privy to just about everything being invented in the computer industry. He eventually left Apple to create his own company, appropriately named Be. Gassée believes the technology explosion in learning allows us to clarify our real goals.

> In our enthusiasm for new learning technologies, we come back to the essential question, What is the goal? For me there can only be one answer: to realize ourselves. To reach this goal requires a kind of learning we never talk about when we are involved in learning technology—knowing yourself. There are quite simply times when you need a master or mentor to learn. Companies need managers because companies are made up of human beings. We need role models, experiences, feelings, relationships, desires. We need someone to look at us and to judge us. Companies that do not have this have no wisdom. Life in these companies can only be, to paraphrase Hobbes, brutal, nasty, and short.[2]

In terms of formal learning, educator Lewis J. Perelman, in his radical manifesto, argues that today's pervasive, "hyperlearning" technologies—everything from Nintendo game players in the kids' room to multimedia computers in the college dorm to powerful, expert systems in industry—have rendered traditional, brick-and-mortar schools obsolete. We live, says Perelman, "in a new knowledge age where active learning impregnates all work and social life." Hidebound educators—and corporate trainers—fail to acknowledge most learning occurs beyond the confines of the classroom. Thanks to everyday tools of the home and workplace, learning "will bear little resemblance to what most people conventionally think of as 'education.'" He writes:

> In the new, posteducation learning enterprise, learning is not only *for* the real world, it is *of* the real world. Not sequestered in the box of a classroom, learning takes place as close as possible to the real-life contexts in which people want learning to be useful. The hyper-learning enterprise is a wide-open community of practice, where learning is by doing, the roles of apprentice and expert are continually shifting with the demands of the problem at hand, learning is self-paced and custom-styled by the individual learner, and passionate—sometimes "spectacular"—learning is motivated by the natural drive of the human brain freed of the fear of failure.[3]

Technology and Action Learning

One version of the future can already be seen at Tsukuba's laboratory for "tele-existence"—similar to virtual reality except technology is used to act in the real world via robots. The tele-existence lab at Tsukuba is strewn with equipment but in the middle is a chair. It looks like a barber's chair with a headset hanging down from a boom at eye level whose main feature is a pair of goggles, as if the apparatus were for testing the eyes. On the right armrest is a glove with wires coming out of it. It's not very reassuring. Cables run between the chair, and a small robot is a short distance in front of it. A young research assistant with a white smock invites you to take the chair.

Placing the goggles before your eyes you get the same reaction you get when you watch a monitor in a store window: among the people dumbly staring at the store window, you are surprised to see yourself. Only now you are projected out of your body and into the little robot in front of your chair! It is very easy—natural, in fact.

And it doesn't take much imagination to think the glove extends your arm into another dimension... and one of these days there will be a whole suit. This means that a lot of what you consider to be yourself can one day be projected out of your body into the heart of a nuclear reactor, say, or on a space dock, or even into a microscopic robot to do surgery. The virtual reality example reminds us technology can be used for active learning in the real world, even though the learning experience is synthesized. Technology and learning are not limited to an artificial electronic world. To be blunt, if you haven't got a plan for phasing technology into your learning strategy, you're shortchanging your future.

Mentoring with Technology

In today's learning organizations, linking wisdom to technology is vital. How do these two resources fit together? Diacom Technologies, a software start-up in Scotts Valley, California, has tried to answer that question. Diacom has created what could well become a new software standard for learning, based on continuous, real-time feedback.

David Boulton founded the company in 1992 with the aim of creating a technological environment for individuals that would sustain their motivation to learn, by giving learners a structure for navigating through text, images, and sound. The design of the system was based on Boulton's observations of his son and friends playing Nintendo games. How did these kids stay engaged? What motivated them to work through a game for hours, making mistakes and learning as fast as they could to reach a more advanced level of play? Boulton's keen insight was that kids had a tacit trust in the game. They knew the resources were there to overcome the obstacles; all they had to do was find them. They were challenged, but had an amazing ability to overcome the frustration of making mistakes and losing games.

What makes Diacom's software such fun is that it accesses different types of information as fast as a video game. It also allows learners to leave messages and gives them feedback when they have a question, suggestion, or problem. This feedback mechanism allows those responsible for the development of learning materials to constantly monitor how learners are doing and understand where they are encountering difficulties. In their work for business organizations, Diacom addresses three significant requirements of technology:

1. Gathering as much feedback as possible from everyone in the organization via telephone- and computer-based information collection
2. Putting mentors in ongoing contact with learners
3. Helping mentors make sense of the high volume of feedback an organization generates

Putting coaches, mentors, and information providers on-line is useful not only for learning but also for teams making a product— Diacom is working with project teams from a large aerospace firm— as well as for quality improvement systems, management information reporting, and employee communication. Says Boulton, "I'm concerned with developing a world that's dialogue friendly."

Boulton started Diacom with a vision of how learning should be supported as the essential human resource for society. Ten years earlier, he was president of Dynapro, a robotics company that was very successful but made him miserable. He didn't like having people seek his favor or consent, and he didn't like the rigorous time management needed to keep two shifts of workers building robots; above all, he didn't like finding himself in the position of manipulating people. So he left the company and went off on what he called a "learning binge" for a year: he read, traveled, and avidly devoted himself to learning anything he wanted—psychology, religion, archeology, whatever. That experience allowed him to trust his own learning process. He would start a book on physics, stop when he felt like it, and come back to finish it months later, having explored other realms of wisdom that were seemingly unconnected but fit together as he continued his journey.

What struck Boulton was that this trust in his own learning process was new to him, something that had been drummed out of him since his first days in school. Yet this trust was the real key to learning. He explains:

> I had grown up with the notion that somebody out there knows what I don't know. In my learning binge, that belief crashed. I discovered that in any field of knowledge that I pursued, I would get to an edge where the experts were carrying on a raging war about what was true. It hit me that the universe is wide open and that there is always a fluctuating edge to knowledge. That was a truly liberating experience.
>
> At the same time, I became irritated with what I call the insidious curriculum of education. We learn from the first days in school that it is not our own impulse to inquire that counts, what's really important is following the lesson. I discovered that the reality of learning is just the opposite. What's really important is the activity of learning and our own impulses and questions. When a child learns to walk, it does not "acquire a skill," it extends its being in space. When that child grows older and learns geometry in school he or she does not acquire a "subject" but extends his or her mental being into an abstract realm of space. And out on the edge of that realm, there is a fluctuating limit to the learner's being that constitutes what is to be explored.[4]

The importance of Boulton's approach is that it is responsive; it does not assume "this is what you need at this time," an assumption implicit in education systems, corporate training programs, and most learning technology. Diacom's technology accommodates the fluctuating needs of the learner.

Boulton finds it dangerous to assume "educators" can accurately predict how an individual should learn best. Not only is that assumption untrue, but it also cuts off the individual from taking control of learning.

Boulton calls authentic learning activity "semnastics" from the Greek for exercise of meaning. Learning, he says, is like a sport that one plays or practices. Technology should support semnastics. Like a game, technology should allow learners to go as fast as they can and stay out on the edge where they are excited. They should be able to slow down, make mistakes, and get help from coaches, as they would during sports practice.

One of Diacom's early experiments with its technology was with second- and third-grade classes in Cupertino, California. Diacom technologists and classroom teachers decided to offer the kids the opportunity to explore economics, a subject that would support Boulton's fundamental belief that anybody can learn anything. They decided to study corn as a vehicle for learning economics. For two weeks, the teachers gathered information and entered it into a computer—how corn is produced, cultivated, processed, and so on.

When the program was offered to the students, Boulton turned on the computer and explained the on-screen icons they could use to navigate through the program. Down the side of the screen were buttons that allowed them to go forward or back through the lesson; there was also an important button that allowed the kids to dialogue with the teacher. Other buttons let the kids get dictionary definitions, hear stories, or get more information. Then Boulton turned the kids loose, three to a computer. Underlying the learning process was a learning construct called economics.

The result astounded the teachers and the programmers. It took five minutes, no more, for the second- and third-graders to familiarize themselves with the system and figure out how to study corn in a way that was natural to them. The teachers said that to get the same familiarity in a normal teaching setting with books and home-work would take more than two weeks!

Clever technology aside, Diacom's real breakthrough is recognizing the human dimension of accompaniment through dialogue. Although it has an important place in learning, technology itself doesn't of itself drive learning or abet wisdom. As Boulton reminds us: "The problem isn't even one of cost. Systems capable of totally transforming our relationship with information, of providing a new (learner) interface to recorded knowledge, will ultimately prove to be very cost-effective. But so long as the role of educational technology is viewed in terms of isolated subject mastery rather than as *a mediator of a new general relationship*... its force in educational evolution will remain misdirected."[5]

13

. . . .

The Policy Imperative

None of us—as members of an organization, a family, or a community—can afford to ignore the greater learning needs of our society. No nation can content itself with only average learning in workplaces or schools.

This is especially true of the wealthy workforces of North America, Western Europe, and Japan, which now compete head-on with more than a billion workers in China, India, the Pacific Rim, Eastern Europe, and South America who are starting to make the same goods with the same skills. Leaders in every country see that a low-skill workforce equals a low-wage workforce and that the level of skill necessary to compete globally is constantly increasing. The developing nations are learning to learn with surprising speed.

Take Singapore. Former Prime Minister Lee Kuan Yew, not content to be a follower of the Japanese model, devised a leapfrog strategy of alliances with developed countries. His explicit goal was to develop the world's most competitive workforce—on an island the size of Chicago with a population of 2.8 million. By force of national will and single-minded (indeed, autocratic) leadership, today's Singaporean workforce has been rated the world's best for ten years running by the American Business Environment Risk Information Service.[1] It commands the world's most advanced telecommunications infrastructure, factories, and research facilities, thanks to its partnerships with Apple Computer, AT&T, Digital

Equipment, Deutsche Bank, Hewlett-Packard, IBM, Matsushita, NEC, Philips, and others.

Commitment in the far more difficult context of a diverse, wildly individualistic democracy is needed to meet today's learning challenge in the United States. David Kearns, former CEO of Xerox, estimates that U.S. business will need to spend $25 billion per year on remedial education alone.[2]

Joseph Boyett and Henry Conn outline three reasons why the U.S. workforce is unprepared to meet the education challenge: (1) the growing number of jobs that will require two years of college education as a bare minimum, (2) the failure to bridge the learning gap between school and workplace, and (3) the declining quality of basic education for those who are now in school and who will constitute the first generation of the U.S. workforce in the twenty-first century.[3]

What Role Should Government Play?

Workforce training and retraining is high on the Clinton administration's agenda. Robert Reich, secretary of labor, has announced plans to spend $13 billion for five years to replace the current unemployment insurance system with an overhauled "reemployment" system. (That's in addition to about $6 billion a year in federal job-training efforts.) The Clinton program would provide one-stop career centers, jointly funded by state and federal government— bringing under one roof a maze of programs now spread over many agencies: income support, career counseling and job training, and the use of a planned, nationwide jobs data base.

The Clinton administration's proposed training effort, which calls for up to eighteen months of income assistance for trainees, would extend under a single umbrella three major needs: work-to-work programs (for displaced or vulnerable workers), school-to-work (for those entering the workforce), and welfare-to-work.

Reich's attempt to reinvent traditional job-training programs included a proposal to allow private sector competition to the federal employment service. Government retraining funds would go to the entity—public, private, academic, or collaborative effort—that produced results. The career centers would further prove their worth by selling their services to employers, students, or workers who are ineligible for public retraining assistance but willing to pay for the services offered. Late in 1994, Congress tabled the plan, but Clinton has since proposed the elimination of some sixty job-training programs, with the $10 to $13 billion annual savings given directly to individuals in the form of vouchers. This would allow employed and unemployed workers to purchase their own training, and would fuel demand for effective training strategies.

As another part of the training effort, Reich champions a European-style apprenticeship program to provide job training for the 75 percent of U.S. youth who don't earn a four-year college degree. The program would tightly link workplace training, under the guidance of a job-site mentor, with at least a year of school-based learning, leading to a certificate of accomplishment in a presumably marketable skill. "Europe does a far better job than we do in investing in its workers, particularly at the lower end of the socio-economic ladder," says Reich. "In Germany, you have apprenticeship programs that are unrivaled. You have in other European countries a greater degree of collaboration between schools and employers. Employers are doing a much better job than in the United States providing on-the-job training."[4]

Yet despite the laudable goals and the proposed financial investment, the cost of the retraining efforts envisioned by Reich could run to a staggering $1.6 trillion—nearly 100 times the amount initially budgeted—according to University of Chicago labor economist James Heckman.[5] And there is little evidence massive spending will create the workforce the United States needs to maintain its competitive advantage. Although focused job-search assistance—including skill assessments, job-search workshops, and individual counseling—does pay off, the addition of expensive retraining programs doesn't show commensurate benefits to displaced workers. Indeed, evaluations of the federal Trade Adjustment Assistance Program (for workers displaced by global competition) have shown extensive retraining has actually depressed the total earnings of displaced workers by prolonging their unemployment spells without improving their earnings when they do return to work.[6]

University of Chicago economist Robert J. LaLonde, who has studied the costs of worker dislocation, says, "There is little empirical evidence that intensive retraining efforts really work for displaced workers. The one thing that does seem effective is simple job-search assistance and counseling. It doesn't cost much and is therefore cost-effective. But there needs to be evaluation and experimentation with lots of different strategies to learn more about what works."[7]

Indeed, although little evidence indicates massive retraining programs have been effective, plenty of evidence suggests that passive learning strategies of the past will not do the job. Extensive retraining efforts benefit only 20 to 30 percent of dislocated workers, according to the federal Office of Technology Assessment. Studies show short-term job-training efforts have done little to improve workers' earnings; the benefits of long-term training are equivocal, at best.[8]

Meanwhile, Europe's apprenticeship programs are under close, critical scrutiny as a possible model for bridging the gap that separates youth from the skills they need to work in meaningful jobs.

Should We Adopt the Apprenticeship System?

Apprenticeship goes back centuries in European history; during the Middle Ages, it constituted the only basis for training craftsmen in the specific skills of their trade—the proverbial butcher, baker, and candlestick maker. These craftsmen organized themselves into guilds that preserved the exclusive right of members to exercise a trade; town charters specified no one from a neighboring village would be allowed to compete, and the candlestick maker could not do a little butchering or baking on the side to supplement his income. The apprenticeship system was part and parcel to feudalism: beyond teaching skills to young workers, it regulated the professions and protected professionals from competition—including competition from their own apprentices!

Typically, a youth's family would sign a contract with a master craftsman when the apprentice reached the age of twelve; thereafter, he would live with his master, who would play the role of a substitute father to whom he owed loyalty, obedience, and respect. Rare was the apprentice who himself rose to become a member of a guild (the expectation of upward mobility is a modern invention). No wonder so many fled the system during the companion movement of the eleventh century.

But when industrialization in Europe brought about an explosion of new techniques for making things on a mass scale, it undermined the unchanging and secretive know-how of the master craftsmen and their domination of work; industry made the guilds irrelevant and provided new skills to workers who were mainly from the peasantry.

As a system of education, apprenticeship came to be despised by Europe's new political thinkers, who promoted public education for all; they saw apprenticeship as a system for exploiting workers and limiting the spread of knowledge. That's why apprenticeship was banned in France after the French Revolution and never took root in the new American colonies; many of the colonists were only too relieved to have escaped the system in Europe. In the new nation-states, it became a commonly held right for any person to exercise the trade he or she chose.

In Germany, however, apprenticeship was transformed for technical training in industry. Many companies adopted the apprenticeship system in the early 1900s after August Borsig showed the superiority of his invention, a *lehring system*, in which young industrial workers would be alternatively trained in practical skills on the factory floor and instructed in technical principles in a classroom. Thus began a tradition specific to the Germanic and Nordic countries where industry and secondary education merged to create a new life for apprenticeship, while the Mediterranean nations— France, Italy, and Spain—maintained a strictly academic school system.

In today's Europe of high unemployment, the German system offers clear advantages for integrating youth into work organizations. In France, for example, fully one-quarter of the three million unemployed—13 percent of the workforce—are between the ages of sixteen and twenty-five; on the other side of the Rhine, that number is only 4 percent.[9] That's because more than two-thirds of German youth opt for time-sharing apprenticeships, which allow them to learn any of 374 trades while they finish secondary school.

It is an open question as to how successfully and quickly this system can be transplanted to a more generalist educational system. Only one French company in ten takes on apprentices, and these are mostly small craft businesses or family-owned stores that need cheap labor. By contrast, German companies spend four times more on apprenticeship than on continuing training, and practically all large companies have extensive programs for educating apprentices.

But it may be legitimately asked whether a system that has done an excellent job of training skilled industrial workers is adapted to the needs of a postindustrial workforce. German leaders are in the throes of self-doubt about their highly developed industrial base, which is the most costly and perhaps least flexible in the world. Manufacturing jobs are leaving for countries with lower wages or more flexible labor laws—Mercedes-Benz is setting up a major factory in the United States, and BMW is moving manufacturing to the United Kingdom. Indeed, no major German automaker has plans to open new factories in Germany. If workers need to maintain their own employability by moving from career to career, the apprenticeship system is going to need much retooling before it becomes synonymous with flexibility and individual responsibility.

The nub of the educational dilemma for the United States: on the one hand, an unmanaged transition from education to the workplace leaves an unacceptable number of casualties, especially when unemployment is high; on the other hand, the apprenticeship model's tightly managed transition from school to work tends to stifle flexibility and entrepreneurship. After all we have said about the need for multiple learning paths for adults, we can only agree with learning theorist Patricia Cross who writes: "I believe that the single most important goal for educators at all levels and in all agencies of the learning society is the development of lifelong learners who possess the basic skills for learning plus the motivation to pursue a variety of learning interests throughout their lives. There is some danger that the present educational system is geared to creating dependent rather than independent learners."[10]

The solution to our educational dilemma is not a wholesale embrace of systems from abroad, however effective they may be in their own culture. Although local communities and policymakers seek answers for America's troubled K-12 system, higher education in the United States is still second to none. Business and education leaders are also finding it is our most useful platform for developing a competitive advantage in learning. The elements of a higher education strategy for the workplace include:

- Personal responsibility and career flexibility

- An infrastructure of community college/business partnerships

- A cost-effective local approach allowing for experimentation rather than a centralized, uniform effort.

These elements are coming together in a new model that combines:

- Specific company and industry training programs

- Entrepreneurial expertise and capital

- Community college staff and resources

- Networks of workers—in forms still to be invented—
  analogous to local labor organizations and chambers of
  commerce

This model points to a strategic learning alliance of campuses
linked to the local community, business, and education to provide
needed workforce services. At the same time, it allows serious self-
learning and change-learning—something European apprenticeship programs do not achieve.

Learning strategists in organizations can, in our view, play a significant role in building the twenty-first-century U.S. workforce.
Government alone cannot solve the problem because the wisdom
needed for workers is in our companies and in our educational
system. We should not try to import systems from other countries
because they draw on deep resources within their own cultures.
Leveraging wisdom on a public policy scale requires strategic alliances linking our best and most dynamic institutions. We shall see
how some organizations are pointing the way in Chapter Fourteen.

. . . .

The Partnership Imperative

Community colleges working in partnership with large and small companies equipped with new multimedia software have begun to provide a unique and effective infrastructure for massive learning. Hundreds of technical and community colleges and a handful of four-year schools now work with local businesses to provide cost-effective educational resources far beyond the reach of most companies.

A leader in workplace training is Regis University, a Denver-based Jesuit institution that has sponsored vibrant entrepreneurial ventures to expand its learning mission.[1] The Regis Corporate Partnerships program provides custom training and development under contract to local businesses and unions. The key to the program is Regis's staff of on-site program directors, who manage the learning needs of the client's workforce. They operate as full-time learning managers immersed in the culture of the client firm, but maintain an outsider's perspective. To keep their flexibility and independence, the directors are paid by Regis and manage their own training budgets. The directors, like internal general managers, are largely free of corporate hierarchy and don't have to seek dozens of sign-offs; they can respond quickly to the changing work climate, with the insight of those who know the company from the inside out.

The on-site directors move freely throughout their client organizations to identify needs and develop programs, provide one-on-one job counseling, and champion learning at the worksite. The directors also bring in resources from the college or elsewhere in the community, and provide a link between their client organizations and the world of academia. Employees have free access to the school's library and student services and can apply their workplace training toward a college or postgraduate degree from Regis (as well as in-company certificate programs). Regis, in turn, has recruited several client executives as part-time faculty and has used the real-world experience of its clients' executives to deliver and help develop more courses in change, leadership, and corporate culture.

The program passes the test of any true partnership: it has thoroughly intertwined the operations of both entities, all but erasing the distinction between school and company. For instance, Kathy Bartlett has worked as on-site director of the Regis partnership with Coors Brewing Co. since 1990. She says she performs three critical functions inside the company:

1. Employee advocate, encouraging workers to return to school or otherwise develop their careers

2. Participant in the functions of Coors's organizational development department

3. Developer of new employee-education programs

Bartlett operates as a high-level learning strategist, with wider range and greater access to top management than most of her corporate counterparts. For example, in late 1993, Coors offered voluntary severance packages that resulted in more than 600 early retirements—about 10 percent of Coors managers. As a trusted, informed, and impartial career adviser, Bartlett was sought by some of the company's most senior managers, many of whom opted to leave. "Suddenly people needed a sounding board to help them assess their skills and experience and make the right decision," she says.

The success of the Regis partnership led Peter Coors, vice chairman and CEO, and Leo Kiely, president and chief operating officer, to ask Bartlett to develop two new programs to spearhead continued change efforts: a performance-management program to help people direct and assess much of their own work; and a mentoring program, which took off after she put Coors managers in touch with counterparts at other firms who had created similar programs.

As a learning strategist, Bartlett is directly accountable to the top leadership of the company for workforce development—clearly signaling to people at all levels that personal and professional learning is a critical strategic issue. And she provides those services cost-effectively. One company estimate shows a three-to-one return on investment for the Coors/Regis partnership.

The on-site directors provide "leading-edge, R&D services to the client," says Susan Kannel, Regis University director of corporate partnerships. But it's a role that has to be learned. "Responding to the needs of the business and maintaining the independence of an academic can be a difficult balancing act," she admits. The directors' academic position assures their autonomy, but offers lower pay; their corporate affiliation affords first-rate facilities and resources, but demands long workdays and tough performance standards.

Motorola University

Motorola University, perhaps the world's premier corporate training program, has helped 130,000 Motorola employees, suppliers, and customers learn a wide spectrum of disciplines, from engineering to human resource management and personal leadership.

Motorola University is designed as a "center for strategic thinking and a major catalyst for change," says Dave Basarab, manager of evaluation. The university is the result of a realization in the early 1980s that, to compete globally, "we had to rewrite the rules of corporate training and education," writes William Wiggenhorn, vice president of training and education and president of Motorola University. "Change had to be continuous and participative, and... education—not just instruction—was the only way to make all this occur."[2] The effort required an unwavering commitment from the top. (To dramatize the importance he placed on the firm's quality-training program, then-CEO Bob Galvin asked his top managers to begin their monthly meetings with their quality reports; he then left before the financial results were presented.)

The university's instructional system designers are accorded the full status of senior product engineers (department chairs, in the academic world). Motorola defines the strategic direction for learning within the company and teaches key "relational skills": customer satisfaction, manufacturing supervision, negotiation, and communication. Motorola's training partners at community colleges and trade schools throughout the world develop and deliver much of the training in technical and business skills — math, electronics, statistical process control, and so on.

Motorola University has no full-time faculty; those positions are subcontracted to colleges, independent trainers, and Motorola employees who share their expertise while on temporary assignment to the university. Training methodology ranges from classroom training led by professional teachers to original course work developed by line managers to, in the business units themselves, the "embedded learning" of shop-floor workers teaching their peers essential job skills. (One manager in a semiconductor-testing department delivers his own sixteen-week leadership-development course for employees at all levels.)

Underlining the strategic importance of learning, Motorola University has its own board of trustees, which includes CEO Gary Tooker, President Christopher Galvin, and the heads of the company's major businesses. Like the rest of the company, Motorola University rigorously—perhaps obsessively—measures its results. Basarab cites an average return on investment of 30:1 attributable to training. From 1987, when Motorola University began rolling out the company's "six sigma" quality initiative, to 1993, productivity jumped 126 percent companywide—an indication of the impact of the company's massive commitment to employee development.

Motorola University holds all courses to consistent standards of effectiveness based on a four-point scale developed by trainer Donald Kirkpatrick:[3]

Level 1: participant satisfaction with the instructor, materials, and setting. To pass muster, every course must show continuous improvement in participant satisfaction rates.

Level 2: mastery of learning objectives and assimilation of new knowledge. Participants take self-administered tests to grade the course, not the individual. To be successful, a course must show that 80 percent of participants have mastered carefully targeted learning objectives.

Level 3: transfer of knowledge and skills to the job. University personnel work with business unit managers to determine whether classroom knowledge (in a selective sample of courses) is being applied to the job. If not, the managers and their university colleagues determine why not.

Level 4: demonstrated business results of training. Though a previous evaluation estimates the 30:1 return on overall investment, Motorola has not yet calculated hard-dollar results for specific courses. Such measures will be the focus of future learning evaluations.

Motorola University has gone far beyond other learning organizations in addressing the difficult Level 3 measures—and in involving managers and other stakeholders in facilitating learning. The key, says Basarab, is having unit managers identify critical skills and then decide how best to support their learning goals. "They look at what factors inhibit or promote the transfer of learning to the workplace," he says. "The managers themselves define what are the most critical skills necessary for success and what obstacles need to be removed to make the necessary fixes in the workplace."

But the real benefit goes beyond the bottom line. "The university was chartered to be a change agent," says Ray Waddoups, vice president of Motorola University and director of Motorola University West. "Our mission is to lead the corporation to a new culture of lifelong learning and develop new methods necessary for success in global competition." Training is developed to support specific strategic objectives, such as improved cycle times or reduced waste. Waddoups cites, for example, a design-for-manufacturability course he championed for two thousand engineers in the company's government and defense unit. Despite initial resistance from managers who resented giving up their engineers for two days of training, the course achieved major breakthroughs in design engineering and led Motorola's defense sector to higher quality manufacturing. "The training changed the culture of that organization," insists Waddoups. "It was a push into the future."[4]

The lesson, from high-performing companies like Motorola, Raychem, and others, is that sustained technical excellence—and hence competitiveness—relies on the continuous professional development of all hands. Thus, every employee is expected to pursue learning, and managers are held accountable not just for meeting strategic goals and shipping products, but also for directing, assessing, and enhancing the learning of those they manage. For ultimately, these companies know continuous learning *is* strategy.

A Look at the Future

Tomorrow, education will necessarily sell learning and will distribute personalized services throughout the human life cycle. Learners will be consumers whose demands will constitute business opportunities. Already Club Med, world leader in the leisure resort industry, is designing learning centers to replace the "sun, sea, and sex" market of the 1970s.

In the learning institutions of the future, costs and overheads will be cut to a minimum to provide maximum value. Communication and assessment will be much better organized. There will be all the familiar marketing techniques for attracting and keeping customers: advertising, brand names, frequent-user coupons, economy packages, year-end sales...junk mail in every mailbox.

Future innovations will most likely come in the form of new resources built to serve learning institutions networked in partnerships and alliances.

One example is an alliance between student communities and universities, a start-up launched under the name Metizo (from the Greek *ethidzo,* learning by imitation, and *meta,* superior form of learning).[5] Metizo consults, designs, and provides learning programs in residential learning centers that add to their regular studies. Metizo guides seventeen- to twenty-five-year-old students toward an active life via self-development, teamwork, and "learning to learn." The program targets three key areas:

1. *Learning efficiency.* Students progress in their studies and in managing their entry into a career by
   - learning to set goals and priorities, first in formal education and later in choosing a career and finding a job;
   - mastering information and learning tools, especially computers and networks;
   - gaining experience in cooperation and teamwork; and
   - building a personal health program for maintaining physical and psychological balance.
2. *Experience.* Students learn skills useful for active life by
   - acquiring experience in problem solving, negotiation, debate, and other skills;

- learning in a team environment and mastering team dynamics and leadership roles; and

- completing annual investigative missions lasting at least two weeks—the first year in difficult working conditions, the second year in a country undergoing social conflict, and the third year working in a humanitarian aid program.

3. *Awareness*. Students reach a state of self-knowledge and autonomy enabling them to choose the career path best suited to their personality, talents, and aspirations. They define their social commitments through

- self-discovery, examination, discussion, and application of their beliefs, values, and ideals;

- self-testing through questionnaires, interviews, games, and so forth; and

- self-expression and creativity supported by a learning community.

During their stay, students learn from one another, in teams formed around a variety of learning projects. They can also draw on the international network of students and teachers linked by computer and the personal guidance of experts from affiliated schools and businesses.

Whether student residences, a company that works with the government to renew job skills, or a corporate university, developing people is a partnering process.

When the structure of social and commercial organizations is being questioned as never before, one mission is essential—the promotion and delivery of learning to every constituent. Achieving that goal means fundamentally rethinking the boundaries that have governed our Industrial Age institutions.

Conclusion

. . . .

Working Wisdom

We've seen how people work with wisdom as learners, tacticians, and strategists in organizations throughout the world. Running like a thread through these stories, wisdom animates relationships in the learning organization and gives new meaning to an old word. We've seen that wisdom is a resource available to anyone willing to invest in his or her own development and draw lessons from experience. Just as importantly, we've seen how wisdom assumes economic and strategic value in today's organizations.

The Wisdom of Leaders

Jim Kouzes, chairman and CEO of The Tom Peters Group/Learning Systems, and Barry Posner, professor of organizational behavior, have rigorously studied the foundations of leadership; several of their findings have important parallels for the application of wisdom in the workplace. True leadership, they write, is built on a relationship, not between bosses and subordinates, but between leaders and constituents in a community of interest. Likewise, we see that wisdom is not passed from an authoritarian teacher to a supplicant student, but is discovered in a learning relationship in which both stand to gain a greater understanding of the workplace and the world. The stories of Diana Edwards, Dennis Luther, and

Reto Wittwer, among others, show the power of learning relationships in building not only leadership but also wisdom.

Kouzes and Posner also describe a process of self-discovery, arrived at through mastery and leading to personal credibility, just as it leads to wisdom; they find credible leaders "develop the capacity of people in the organization to act on...shared values and expand or realize the potentialities of the people in the organizations they lead."[1] They do this by providing necessary resources and investing themselves in the learning process.

Kouzes and Posner also have studied techniques for delivering a message. They tell managers to look for "teachable moments," significant points in the life of an organization or individual that lend themselves to a shared understanding. For example, Leon Royer constantly finds teachable moments in a catalytic story about a lost customer or—to show his commitment to quality—the public acknowledgment of a shop-floor worker who stops the production line when she spots a problem.

Working Wisdom

To tap people's potential to learn, leaders can target seven areas of action available to most organizations:

1. *Coherent learning strategy.* This requires committed and visible learning leaders: Matsushita, Bob Galvin of Motorola, Kuni-yasu Sakai of Bunsha Group, Guichard of Casino, Dubrule and Pélisson of Accor. At the national policy level, Bob Reich has certainly been a visible leader with a strategy, recognized as a major influence in international policy making for developed countries.

2. *Mentors, coaches, and learning managers.* People within an organization need to take responsibility for learning and effec-

tively transfer wisdom by understanding how to motivate, support, and accompany learners.

3. *Effective learning tactics.* Five ways to use wisdom to help others learn have been identified and examined in detail: accompanying, sowing, catalyzing, showing, and harvesting. These tactics make the learning relationship work when adapted to suit personal styles and learners' needs.

4. *Contracts for learning in work.* Career development is no longer a matter of climbing the rungs of the corporate ladder. It's a matter of continuous learning. The new work contract has the salutary effect of putting individual responsibility for learning into focus. It creates a benchmark for the value of managers in enhancing work—and a standard for the employee in contributing to value.

5. *Learning to learn.* Education is not the end of learning to learn; special effort must be made for less educated workers to acquire the skills of continuous learning. This is a fundamental management task as we try to accommodate a diverse workforce. The growth of corporate universities—from 85-employee ICC to 100,000-employee Motorola suggests that employers recognize the need to develop the learning capacity of every employee.

6. *Cross-Learning.* This learning is essential in the collaborative networks and cross-functional teams prevalent in many organizations we've seen, from the Counsel Connect network to Dun & Bradstreet's front-line facilitators. Learning leaders, mentors, and coaches enhance team performance by maintaining motivation to learn, confronting learning problems, and orchestrating a learning exchange.

7. *Unlearning.* Some things we learn are either ineffective or obsolete and must be unlearned. Wise managers provide the support and guidance necessary to discard old learning, often

integrated deeply into habits and beliefs. Unlearning, in other words, is *learning to change*—and constitutes the most valuable application of wisdom. We've seen how sowers, catalyzers, and leaders in many of the organizations studied have successfully brought together personal development and organizational change.

Managers—if they assume the responsibility of wisdom—are in an ideal position to make the learning organization a reality. There is really no objective way of determining if a manager has earned the right to exercise wisdom; today's organizations have no initiation rites or ceremonies as many traditional societies do. The "right" to work with wisdom is a personal commitment as much as the embodiment of a new role within the organization. There is a price: we have to ask ourselves deep questions; we have to take the risk of revealing ourselves in an authentic learning relationship.

Today's learning needs are immense. According to a work ethic only now emerging, employees take responsibility for their own development and learn how to learn. At the same time, it is obvious not everyone is completely autonomous; not all of us have the skills and resources we need. None of us has achieved sufficient wisdom to stop learning: we need others.

Our conclusion is perfectly formulated in three lines of poetry written in the eighteenth century by William Blake. These lines were quoted at a commemoration of one of the most powerful teachers of our time, R. D. Laing, shortly after his death.

> The angel that presided o'er my birth
> Said: Little creature, made of joy and mirth,
> Go love without the help of anything on earth.[2]

The lines remind us that there is a golden chain of wisdom that links the generations. These links are moments of love—or perhaps love manifested at certain moments.

What each of us has learned as an adult depends on the simple fact that someone has loved us enough to make a commitment, for a time, to our future. A benefactor puts wisdom at our service as a gift, a gift all the more precious because it can never be repaid to its donor. All we can do is pass these gifts on by becoming wise and making our wisdom useful enough to be learned by others.

Appendix

. . . .

A Brief History of
Working Wisdom

If wisdom has not been considered relevant to the work of managers, it is because we have lost a clear notion of its use in industrial societies. This is particularly true in the United States. It is widely recognized that our present educational systems are not fulfilling the responsibility of educating for life. In fact, even the most essential learning institution, the family, is not providing a sufficient basis for the education of children, despite parental efforts. In all developed countries, schools and the family as social institutions need help dealing with the complex problems of change we face today. Because of a curious knot of history, the institution most responsible for providing individuals with wisdom geared to the needs of postindustrial society is the work organization. The organization, particularly the knowledge-based organization, must become a model in managing working wisdom.

But appreciating wisdom, let alone managing it, is not easy. The paradigms that dominate the Western mindset make the very idea of working wisdom strange. The discomfort is cultural, going back to the origins of the Western concept of wisdom. To a large extent, the European intellectual tradition portrays the person of action as a moral outcast, an intellectual intruder, a brute who must be governed by ethical codes and religions. These people seem to have no legitimate wisdom of their own.

An education in wisdom for managers should therefore include some examination of what wisdom is and why we have misunderstood it until now. Let's briefly examine the issue.

Scrutinizing the history of wisdom in the West, we find a first parting of the ways in the fifth century B.C., when Plato declared that wisdom, *sophia,* was an eternal and unchangeable superior knowledge acquired only through philosophy. The famous dialogue from Plato's *Gorgias* summarizes the fundamental conflict in our understanding of wisdom.

The Western Battle of Wisdom

One of Plato's early dialogues, Gorgias represents the turning point in the Greek contest over wisdom. This is the first time in Greek culture that the wisdom of a man of action is clearly denigrated. Gorgias, after whom the dialogue is named, was a famous sophist and teacher of rhetoric. In the dialogue that Plato imagines—we know the conversation historically could not have taken place because the characters lived in different generations—Socrates and Gorgias are invited to the home of Callicles, a wealthy Athenian man of affairs.

Socrates and Gorgias open the conversation by debating whether rhetoric can be taught. Very early on, Gorgias withdraws from the debate and leaves the argument to a younger disciple. But as the disciple quickly loses ground the true man of action, Callicles, steps in. This is the point at which Plato becomes deadly serious. The argument soon turns to a duel in which each questions the value and legitimacy of the other's way of life.

Socrates claims the essence of wisdom is in questioning the important values of culture. Callicles retorts that wisdom comes with experience. Historically, Callicles is known to have claimed a little philosophy was good when one is young, but leads to a dangerous intellectualism if pursued too long as an adult. In Plato's dialogue, Callicles goes much further and accuses Socrates of building a world of dreams and of "whispering his ideas to young men" rather than debating them openly before the people in a democracy. He exhorts Socrates to give up philosophy because it is "spoiling" him.

But Plato weaves a cunning web around the man of action. We find Callicles is forced to defend a theory of justice whereby the stronger naturally has justice on his side. Socrates then comes to the conclusion that Callicles' wisdom, stemming from the exercise of power and the accumulation of experience, is really nothing more than a "form of flattery" whose only goals are pleasure and the approval of others.

The Origins of Working Wisdom

What are the consequences of Plato's self-prescribed victory of intellectual wisdom over the practical? The claim that there is a "true" knowledge of the soul and that only philosophy can determine the ultimate goals of action became the dominant tradition for the West. The lessons of experience and the mastery of worldly affairs became false, and the wisdom of active life was reduced to nothing more than a form of vanity.

Aristotle, at the death of Plato, his teacher and mentor for twenty years, took another decisive step in defining wisdom by providing a hierarchy of the different kinds of wisdom, putting the man of experience near the bottom and the theorist at the top as we see here in the beginning of his *Metaphysics:* "The man of experience is thought to be wiser than the possessors of any sense-perception whatever, the artist wiser than the men of experience, the master-worker than of the mechanic, and the theoretical kinds of knowledge to be more of the nature of Wisdom than the productive. Clearly then Wisdom [*sophia*] is knowledge about certain principles and causes."[2]

It is useful to know the Greeks had two different words for wisdom: *sophia*, used in the above passage, and *phronesis*, which is translated as practical wisdom. Aristotle actually defines the Greek word *phronesis* as the application of experience, and this allowed him to lay the foundations of two major inventions of Western civilization, law and psychology. Though Aristotle extensively explored practical wisdom, he definitively segregated the man of action from the "higher" forms of wisdom.

Practical wisdom continues throughout history, operating below the realm of theoretical philosophy, in the form of morality and ethics, which the Romans did much to perfect. On the one hand, the Stoics, such as Seneca, cultivated concepts and techniques to attain an ethic where one experiences the joys and disappointments of human destiny with equanimity. The Epicurians, on the other hand, considered pleasure a positive moral goal. And Roman orators such as Cicero continued the tradition of rhetoric and brought it to perfection as a combination of culture, politics, and education.

Later, with the influence of Christianity, Roman thinkers such as Augustine again rejected *prudentia*, the wisdom of the world, as illusion and vanity. Only *sapentia*, the Latin word for *sophia*, opened the gates to Augustine's City of God.

The Middle Ages developed a society separated into peasants, craftsmen, merchants, knights, and clergy. Only the latter, having taken over the prerogative of the philosophers, adding to it divine faith, could claim access to *sapentia*. It would take a thousand years for Europe to reconsider the hierarchy of wisdom. It was not until the fifteenth century that a rebirth, the Renaissance, successfully overturned the clerical claim to wisdom. The impertinence of Leonardo da Vinci's phrase, "Wisdom is the daughter of experience," should not escape us: it is a radical declaration for his time.

During a little more than a century, Renaissance thinkers began developing a new approach to wisdom based on a philosophy of humanism. A famous debate of this period pitted Cardinal Jacopo Sadoleto against Tommaso Fedro Inghirami, librarian of the Vatican. For Sadoleto, wisdom was contemplative, immutable, and of divine inspiration. For Inghirami, such a philosophy was bereft

of both body and soul; wisdom, rather, consisted in acting with
prudentia, courage, diligence, and honor. He asserted the primary
duty of the sage was to bring honor to his period of history and, in
fact, to change with the times.

The most famous Renaissance book on wisdom actually defined
the new *Working Wisdom*. The book was published in 1604 by the
Frenchman Pierre Charron, *De la Sagesse* (Of Wisdom). In it, he
specifically refutes the transcendentalism of the church and goes so
far as to write of *sapentia:* "I hold it far below prudence, health,
sagacity, virtue and even farther below skill in affairs."[3]

If wisdom was indeed a project of the Renaissance, we should
not be surprised to be affected by it today. The warp, however, can
be explained by the onslaught of the seventeenth-century Enlightenment against Renaissance humanism. The Enlightenment
reestablished a new form of *sophia* as the queen of wisdom—
crowning her now with rationalism and the scientific method.
Francis Bacon was pivotal in defining the method of scientific in-
vestigation that would become the paramount means of discover-
ing truth while René Descartes established the rationalism of the
Modern Age. British empiricists John Locke, George Berkeley, and
David Hume brought further discredit to the *prudentia* of Renaissance wisdom. Thus, by the eighteenth century and the thinking of
François Voltaire, Benedict de Spinoza, and Gottfried Leibniz, Renaissance humanism is as good as buried.

The thinking of the Industrial Revolution, which was based on
these philosophies and a rejection of working wisdom, had decisive
consequences on later management theories. It is well known, for
example, that Taylorism at the beginning of the twentieth century
started from the assumption that management is a science and that
wisdom, particularly the wisdom of workers, should play no part in
it. And though management concepts were later "humanized,"
wisdom was still eliminated from the vocabulary of even the most
people-oriented management theories. The continuing negli-
gence of working wisdom by Western management theory and

education—particularly the MBA—simply compounded Western misunderstanding of experience and learning.

Wisdom in Asian-Pacific Management

Western neglect of wisdom in the managerial realm may have continued to the present day had it not been for the impact of Japanese management theory in the early 1980s. Japanese competitive superiority in the key industries Americans considered their domains of excellence finally provoked a fundamental questioning of U.S. principles and provided an alternative to the mindset that dominated 300 years of industrial thinking.

Japanese management theories opened the door to a serious evaluation of the role wise managers play in organizations. These theories have their own cultural foundation: the Confucian idea of wisdom permeates Japanese management. Confucian wisdom does not accept the Aristotelian distinction between theory and practice. If a Japanese manager is asked about wisdom, he or she will automatically interpret the word in terms a Westerner would call practical wisdom. The same is true for Koreans and for Chinese. Most Japanese can even recite from memory the famous opening lines of the Confucian Analects: "Is it not a pleasure to learn and to repeat or practice from time to time what one has learned?"[4]

Confucius clearly linked learning to wisdom in the fifth century B.C. when he wrote the first book ever on educating adults. Its title is *The Great Learning,* and its goal is to lay the foundations for the making of what he called the "superior man." Wisdom for Confucius takes as its point of departure "work on the self" and progresses through the "extension of learning." This leads necessarily to action, but a superior action because it draws its efficacy from a balanced mind at peace with itself.

Today, the Confucian "superior man," shorn of its male-dominated bias, is the culmination of what any manager, whose cultural reference is the Confucian tradition, can aspire to become.

The point here is not to say Confucian philosophy or Asian management is better than its Western counterparts. Nor is Confucianism the only foundation for management in Asia. Some of the "dragon" countries, such as Thailand, are mostly Buddhist; others, like Brunei and Malaysia, are predominantly Islamic; still others are characterized by a mosaic of underpinnings for managerial wisdom. However, when Western managers are blind to wisdom in their own tradition, they also overlook its importance when they export their management systems abroad, and this is counterproductive in the long run.

Wisdom and Economic Development

By coincidence, while CEOs are redefining the job of the manager, leaders in developing countries are questioning the fundamental values that economic development thrusts upon traditional society. They worry about the effects of materialism and the abandonment of ethical and spiritual concerns among young people. One of Thailand's religious leaders, Phra Rajavaramuni, expresses his disappointment in the management systems Americans have transferred to developing countries. They are techniques without wisdom, he says, that promote economic development while disregarding the basic human needs of personal fulfillment and social progress: "We must find a way to build up a social consciousness for solving problems by having a profound understanding and an interest in a social goal. (And if this is to really do any good you must have an interest in a goal for your own life.) There must be a continuing interest in knowledge, in trying to solve problems successfully through wisdom."[5]

Such concerns are, of course, nothing new; but in a world of confusion following the abrupt end of the Cold War, fundamental questions that were thought to be answered by the superior performance of free market economies take on new meaning. Values and wisdom thus come back into focus as they did in the aftermath of World War II, when Europe and Japan had to rebuild their devastated economies almost from scratch. Today, management is a vehicle for answering the new questions concerning development, a practical way of "solving problems through wisdom."

We need not return to the past; we will not build the values of the learning society by looking in a rearview mirror. To the contrary, we must have the courage to boldly define wisdom in terms of the new economic link between learning and work. Seldom has human society faced such abrupt, profound changes. Indeed, post-industrial society, if it is to improve our lot, may be known as not the Information Age, but as the Age of Wisdom.

Notes

. . . .

Preface

1. Knowles, M. S. *Andragogy in Action*. San Francisco: Jossey-Bass, 1984, p. 6.

Chapter One

1. Knowledge half-life was studied by Hewlett-Packard in the 1980s. This finding for computer engineers was presented by Neil Johnston, formerly corporate training manager for H-P and now president of Orbis Learning Corp., Los Altos, Calif.

2. This distinction was summarized in an interview with the late Claude Mathis, dean of the educational processes department at Northwestern University.

3. First reported in *On Achieving Excellence*. TPG Communications newsletter, September 1993.

4. U.S. Bureau of Labor Statistics. *How Workers Get Their Training: A 1991 Update*. Washington, D.C.: Government Printing Office, pp. 20, 26.

5. Personal interview, Paris, May 1993.

6. A fine description of the Greek idea of culture is provided in Werner Jaeger's master work, *Paideia* (3 vols.). London: Oxford University Press, 1939.

Chapter Two

1. Sakaiya, T. *Chika kakumei*. Kyoto: PHP Kenkyujo, 1985.

2. Sakaiya, T. *The Knowledge-Value Revolution*. (G. Fields and W. March, Trans.). Tokyo: Kodansha, 1991.

3. Sakaiya, T. *The Knowledge-Value Revolution*. (G. Fields and W. March, Trans.). Tokyo: Kodansha, 1991, p. 61.

4. Thanks to Hubert Landier who first introduced Bob Aubrey to this remarkable business leader.

5. Personal interview, Paris, April 1993.

6. Konosuke Matsushita, in a letter explaining why he had established Peace and Happiness through Prosperity, published in the foundation's brochure. PHP studies different cultures, runs management seminars, and publishes books and periodicals.

7. Greco, R. "First Person: From the Classroom to the Corner Office." *Harvard Business Review*, September/October 1992, 5(70), 54–63.

8. Daloz, L. A. *Effective Teaching and Mentoring*. San Francisco: Jossey-Bass, 1990, p. 20.

9. We owe this expression to Ian Browde, who used it as a managerial concept when he was at Apple University.

10. For a description of "process owner," see Hammer, M., and Champy, J. *Reengineering the Corporation*. New York: HarperBusiness, 1993.

11. Personal interview, Scotts Valley, Calif., August 1994.

12. Drucker, P. F. *Adventures of a Bystander*. New York: HarperCollins, 1991, pp. 74–75.

Chapter Three

1. Professor Kaoru Kobayashi helped clarify this shift.

2. Doi, T. *The Anatomy of Self*. Tokyo: Kodansha International Press, 1985, pp. 80–81.

3. Telephone interview, February 1994.

4. Personal interview, Menlo Park, Calif., April 1994.

5. Knowles, M. S. *Using Learning Contracts*. San Francisco: Jossey-Bass, 1986.

6. "Benefits and Costs of Working Freelance." *Financial Times*, April 6, 1990.

7. Jung, C. G. *The Structure and Dynamics of the Psyche, Collected Works*. Vol 8. Princeton: Princeton University Press, Bollinger Foundation, 1960.

8. Erikson, E. "Identity and the Life Cycle." *Psychological Issues*, 1959, 1, 1–171.

9. Levinson, D. *Seasons of a Man's Life*. New York: Ballantine, 1978.

10. Sheehy, G. *Pathfinders*. New York: Bantam, 1981, p. 63.

Chapter Four

1. Site visit, April 1992, and telephone interview, March 1993.

2. Letter to authors, March 26, 1993.

3. Bernard, J. *Le Compagnonnage*. Paris: Presses Universitaires de France, 1972, Preface.

4. Much of this information comes from a conversation on August 29, 1988, with Jean-Pierre Litasse, president of the Order of Minorange, and from subsequent conversations with Bouygues managers. For more information, see Campagnac, E., and Nousille, V. *Citizen Bouygues*. Paris: Editions Belfond, 1988.

5. Michel Bétant began this thinking on the transfer of *compagnonnage* in 1992 with Bouygues's largest project to date, Muang Tong Thani, a new city of one million under construction in Thailand.

6. Personal interview, San Francisco, March 1994.

Chapter Five

1. Shah, I. *The Way of the Sufi*. New York: Penguin, 1974, p. 119.

2. Personal interview, November 1992. See also *On Achieving Excellence*. TPG Communications newsletter, January 1993.

3. Personal interview, September 1989.

4. Telephone interview, February 1993.

5. Telephone interview, February 1993.

6. Telephone interview, March 1993.

Chapter Six

1. Nietzsche, Friedrich. *Beyond Good and Evil*. London: Penguin, 1972, p. 113.

2. During a conversation with a group of French managers on a visit to Sun's headquarters, June 1989.

3. This information was gleaned through many conversations with Reto Wittwer.

Chapter Seven

1. Descartes, R. *Philosophical Essays*. (L. J. Lefleur, Trans.). Indianapolis, Ind.: Bobbs-Merill, 1964, p. 15.

2. Knowles, M. S. *Andragogy in Action*. San Francisco: Jossey-Bass, 1984, pp. 13–14.

3. Knowles calls this nonpedagogical logic of learning "andragogy." The Greek prefix *peda* refers to children; the prefix *andra* refers to adults.

4. Mehta, G. *Karma Cola: Marketing the Mystic East*. New York: Collins/Fontana, 1981, p. 18.

5. The work of Swiss psychologist Jean Piaget, beginning in the 1930s, came to be known as genetic epistemology. It provided a breakthrough in our understanding of infant learning. See Piaget's *Genetic Epistemology*. (E. Duckworth, Trans.). New York: Norton, 1971. Another pioneer of infant imitation is French psychologist Henri Wallon; see his *From Act to Thought* (1942).

6. These are classic experiments in psychology, taken, in this case, from Reuchlin, M. *Psychologie*. Paris: Presses Universitaires de France, 1977.

7. Geert Hofstede makes this point in his study of cultural differences

of management cultures in seventy-two countries, *Les Différences Culturelles dans le Management*. Paris: Editions de l'Organisation, 1987.

8. Personal interview, Evry, France, May 1989.

Chapter Eight

1. Levinson, D. *Seasons of a Man's Life*. New York: Ballantine, 1978, pp. 91–92.

2. McKenna, R. *The Regis Touch*. Reading, Mass.: Addison-Wesley, 1986.

3. Rock, A. "Strategy vs. Tactics: Lessons from a Venture Capitalist." *Harvard Business Review*, November/December 1987, 6(65), 63–67.

4. Jowett edition of "Theatetus." *The Dialogues of Plato*. London: Oxford University Press, 1920, pp. 149–151.

5. Jowett edition of "Theatetus." *The Dialogues of Plato*. London: Oxford University Press, 1920, pp. 149–151.

6. All Sakai quotes from personal interview, November 1989. See also Sakai, K., and Sekiyama, H. *Bunsha*. Tokyo: Tokyo Industries, 1987.

7. All Boyle quotes from telephone interview, February 1994.

8. All Gioia quotes from personal interview, August 1994.

Chapter Nine

1. Personal interview with Pat Canavan, corporate vice president and director of global leadership and organizational development, July 1991.

2. Peters, T., and Waterman, R. *In Search of Excellence*. New York: Harper & Row, 1982, p. 119.

3. Watkins, K. E., and Marsick, V. J. *Sculpting the Learning Organization*. San Francisco: Jossey-Bass, 1993.

4. Telephone interview, April 1994.

5. Schaffer, R. H. *The Breakthrough Strategy*. Cambridge, Mass.: Ballinger, 1988.

Chapter Ten

1. Tichy, N., and Charan, R. "Speed, Simplicity, Self-Confidence: An Interview with Jack Welch." *Harvard Business Review,* September/October 1989, 5(67), 112–120.

2. Personal interviews, April 1994.

3. Personal interview, July 1994.

Chapter Eleven

1. Personal interview, January 1988. Thanks to Ian Browde who recorded the interview.

2. Brill, S. "Scenes from the Next Revolution." *Counsel Connect* newsletter, September 1993.

3. Personal interview with Susan Stucky, IRL associate director, Palo Alto, Calif., August 1994.

Chapter Twelve

1. Personal interview, Paris, February 1990.

2. Personal interview, Paris, February 1990.

3. Perelman, L. J. *School's Out.* New York: Avon, 1992, p. 167.

4. Personal interview, Scotts Valley, Calif., August 1994.

5. Boulton, D. "From Here to Implicity." *California School Boards Journal,* 1990, 67.

Chapter Thirteen

1. Sisodia, R. S. "Singapore Invests in the Nation-Corporation." *Harvard Business Review,* May/June 1992, 3(70), 40–42.

2. Boyett, J. H., and Conn, H. P. *Workplace 2000.* New York: Penguin, 1992, p. 279.

3. Boyett, J. H., and Conn, H. P. *Workplace 2000.* New York: Penguin, 1992, p. 267.

4. Marshall, J. *San Francisco Chronicle,* February 22, 1994, D5.

5. Marshall, J. *San Francisco Chronicle,* February 22, 1994, D5.

6. Mathematica Policy Research, "International Trade and Worker Dislocation: Evaluation of the Trade Adjustment Assistance Program," Princeton, N.J. 1993, pp. 117–124.

7. Telephone interview, March 1994.

8. Marshall, J. *San Francisco Chronicle*, February 22, 1994, D5; see also U.S. Department of Labor. *New Jersey Unemployment Insurance Reemployment Demonstration Project.* Washington, D.C.: Government Printing Office, 1989.

9. Cambon, C., and Butor, P. *La Bataille de l'Apprentissage.* Paris: Descartes & Cie, 1993.

10. Angelo, T. A., and Cross, K. P. *Classroom Assessment Techniques.* San Francisco: Jossey-Bass, 1993, p. 249.

Chapter Fourteen

1. First reported in *On Achieving Excellence.* TPG Communications newsletter, January 1994, with additional telephone interviews, March 1994.

2. Wiggenhorn, W. "Motorola U: When Training Becomes an Education." *Harvard Business Review*, July/August 1990, p. 71.

3. For a complete view of Kirkpatrick's approach, see Kirkpatrick, D. L., *Evaluating Training Programs* (San Francisco: Berrett-Koehler, 1994).

4. Waddoups and Basarab quotes from telephone interviews, March 1994.

5. This organization was started in 1993 by Bob Aubrey to advance experiential learning in education.

Conclusion

1. Kouzes, J., and Posner, B. *Credibility.* San Francisco: Jossey-Bass, 1993, p. 155. See also *The Leadership Challenge* (San Francisco: Jossey-Bass, 1989) by Kouzes and Posner.

2. Blake's poem was quoted by Laing's longtime friend and colleague Francis Huxley at St. James Cathedral, London, January 5, 1990.

Appendix

1. Jowett edition of *The Dialogues of Plato: Gorgias*. London: Oxford University Press, 1920, (vol. 1) pp. 505–591.

2. Aristotle. "Metaphysics, Book I." (W. D. Ross, Trans.). In R. McKeon (ed.), *The Basic Works of Aristotle*. New York: Random House, 1947, pp. 981–982.

3. In fact, few books have been written on wisdom in the history of Western thought. A good overview of wisdom in the Middle Ages and the Renaissance is Rice, E. *The Renaissance Idea of Wisdom*. Cambridge, Mass.: Harvard University Press, 1958. Pierre Charron's quote is on page 182 (translation from the archaic French).

4. Chan, W. T. *A Source Book in Chinese Philosophy*. Princeton, N.J.: Princeton University Press, 1963, pp. 18–47.

5. Rajavaramuni, P. (Prayudh Payutto). *Looking to America to Solve Thailand's Problems*. Bangkok: Sathirakoses-Nagapradipa Foundation, 1987, pp. 5–6.

Recommended Readings

The following list is eclectic; some readings are academic, others are management related, still others are future oriented. The classics—Plato, Aristotle, Confucius—are omitted but are, obviously, recommended as well.

Cross, K. P., *Adults as Learners*. San Francisco: Jossey-Bass, 1992.

Daloz, L. A., *Effective Teaching and Mentoring*. San Francisco: Jossey-Bass, 1990.

de Geus, A., "Planning as Learning," *Harvard Business Review*, March/April 1988, 2(66), 70–72.

Drucker, P. F., *Post-Capitalist Society*. New York: HarperCollins, 1993.

Handy, C., *The Age of Unreason*. Boston: Harvard Business School Press, 1990.

Katzenbach, J. R., and Smith, D. K., *The Wisdom of Teams*. Boston: Harvard Business School Press, 1993.

Knowles, M. S., *The Making of an Adult Educator*. San Francisco: Jossey-Bass, 1989.

Kouzes, J. M., and Posner, B. Z., *Credibility*. San Francisco: Jossey-Bass, 1993.

Levinson, D., *Seasons of a Man's Life*. New York: Ballantine, 1978.

Moore, T., *Care of the Soul*. New York: HarperCollins, 1992.

Nohria, N., and Berkley, J. D., "Whatever Happened to the Take-Charge Manager?" *Harvard Business Review*, January/February 1994, 1(72), 128–137.

Nussbaum, M., *The Fragility of Goodness*. Cambridge, England: Cambridge University Press, 1986.

Perelman, L. J., *School's Out*. New York: Avon, 1992.

Peters, T. *Liberation Management*. New York: Knopf, 1992.

Postman, N., *Technopoly*. New York: Knopf, 1992.

Ross, N. W., *Three Ways of Asian Wisdom*. New York: Simon & Schuster, 1966.

Sakaiya, T., *The Knowledge-Value Revolution*. (G. Fields and W. March, Trans.). Tokyo: Kodansha, 1991.

Senge, P. M., *The Fifth Discipline*. New York: Doubleday/Currency, 1990.

Shah, I., *Learning How to Learn*. New York: Harper & Row, 1981.

Index